# REVISE OCR GCSE (9–1)
# Computer Science
# REVISION GUIDE

Series Consultant: Harry Smith

Author: David Waller

## Also available to support your revision:

The **Revise GCSE Study Skills Guide** is full of tried-and-trusted hints and tips for how to learn more effectively. It gives you techniques to help you achieve your best – throughout your GCSE studies and beyond!

The **Revise GCSE Revision Planner** helps you to plan and organise your time, step-by-step, throughout your GCSE revision. Use this book and wall chart to mastermind your revision.

### Question difficulty

Look at this scale next to each exam-style question. It tells you how difficult the question is.

**For the full range of Pearson revision titles across KS2, KS3, GCSE, Functional Skills, AS/A Level and BTEC visit:**
www.pearsonschools.co.uk/revise

# Contents

......................................

**A small bit of small print**

OCR publishes Sample Assessment Material and the Specification on its website. This is the official content and this book should be used in conjunction with it. The questions in *Now try this* have been written to help you practise every topic in the book. Remember: the real exam questions may not look like this.

# The central processing unit

The central processing unit (CPU) carries out (executes) all of the stored program instructions.

## Components of the CPU

Controls all the other components of the CPU. It contains the **decoder**.

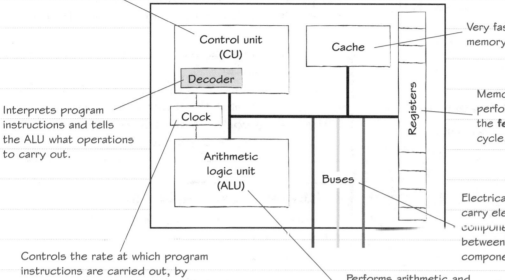

Interprets program instructions and tells the ALU what operations to carry out.

Very fast random access memory (**RAM**).

Memory locations. Some perform special functions in the **fetch–decode–execute** cycle.

Electrical conductors that carry electrical signals between components in the CPU and between the CPU and other components on the motherboard.

Controls the rate at which program instructions are carried out, by sending control electrical signals at regular intervals, called **cycles**.

Performs arithmetic and logical operations to carry out program instructions.

---

 ## Worked example

Matthew has bought a laptop with a 2.2 GHz central processing unit (CPU).

(a) State the purpose of the CPU. **(1 mark)**

The function of the CPU is to fetch and execute program instructions stored in memory.

(b) Describe what is meant by a 2.2 GHz CPU. **(2 marks)**

A 2.2GHz CPU has a clock speed of 2.2 GHz. This gives the number of instructions which can be processed each second. A 2.2 GHz processor can complete 2.2 billion processing cycles per second.

## Clock speed

The CPU carries out one program instruction for each **clock cycle**. Clock speed is usually measured in **gigahertz (GHz)**. 1 GHz is $10^9$ cycles per second. Most home computers have clock speeds between 1 and 3 GHz. The clock speed is one significant factor that affects the performance of the CPU. Other factors include cache size, the number of cores and type of RAM, and hard drive speed.

See page 5 for more about factors which affect the performance of the CPU.

Part (a) uses the word **state** so you do not need to give a detailed description. In part (b), make sure you include at least two distinct statements in your description.

## Now try this

1 List **three** components of a central processing unit (CPU). **(3 marks)**

2 Explain why a computer with a 2.2 GHz CPU might be considered preferable to one with a 1 GHz CPU. **(2 marks)**

# Components of the CPU

The way in which the CPU is designed and carries out the instructions with other components is called 'von Neumann architecture'.

## von Neumann architecture

In 1945, John von Neumann designed a stored program computer where both the program and data are stored in the memory. This is the design we use today.

The components are:

- a processing unit or CPU
- a program counter
- memory to store data and instructions
- input and output mechanisms.

John von Neumann (right) and the stored program computer.

## Control unit

The control unit coordinates the actions of the computer. It sends out control signals to other parts of the CPU and to other components of the computer.

Control signals make everything happen inside a CPU and computer.

An important element is the **decoder**. This works out (decodes) what the program instructions mean. It then sends control signals to other components to carry out the required actions.

## Arithmetic and logic unit

The arithmetic and logic unit (ALU) performs arithmetic and logical operations. It carries out activities such as:

- ✓ addition, subtraction, multiplication and division
- ✓ comparisons between two different numbers.

## Registers used in fetch–decode–execute cycle

**Program counter** – holds the address of the next instruction to be fetched.

**Memory data register** (MDR) – a temporary store (buffer) for anything copied from memory.

### Registers

**Memory address register** (MAR) – holds the address of the memory location currently being read (fetched) or written to.

**Accumulator** – stores the results of calculations carried out by the ALU.

## Worked example

List **two** registers of the CPU with specific functions in the fetch–decode–execute cycle.

**(2 marks)**

Program counter.
Memory address register.

The question asks you to **list** two registers, so no description or explanation is required.

Other registers listed could have been the memory data register and the accumulator.

## Now try this

Describe the role of the control unit in the operation of the central processing unit.

**(4 marks)**

# Fetch-decode-execute cycle 1

The CPU uses the fetch-decode-execute cycle to carry out the program instructions.

## Fetch

During the fetch stage, instructions and data are **transferred from the RAM to the CPU**.

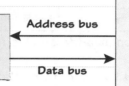

| Random access memory (RAM) | | Central processing unit (CPU) |
|---|---|---|
| Program instructions and data are stored in RAM. | ← Address bus → Data bus | The CPU sends a signal to the RAM requesting the next instruction to be executed. The instruction is sent from the RAM to the CPU. |

## Decode and execute

During the decode and execute stages the instructions are **interpreted and carried out**.

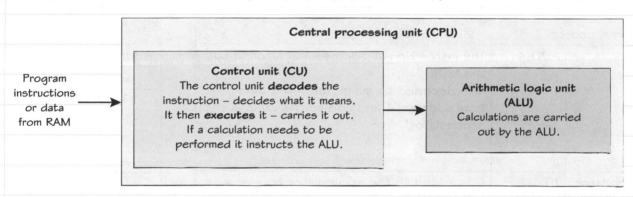

Central processing unit (CPU)

Program instructions or data from RAM →

**Control unit (CU)**
The control unit **decodes** the instruction – decides what it means. It then **executes** it – carries it out. If a calculation needs to be performed it instructs the ALU.

→

**Arithmetic logic unit (ALU)**
Calculations are carried out by the ALU.

---

## Worked example

State what is done at each stage of the fetch–decode–execute cycle. **(3 marks)**

Fetch: The next instruction to be executed is transferred from the RAM to the CPU.

Decode: The CU interprets the instruction.

Execute: The CU then carries out the instruction. It instructs the ALU if calculations need to be performed.

If a question uses the command word 'state' you only need to state your answers, not explain them.

---

## Now try this

Explain how program instructions stored in computer memory are processed by the central processing unit.

**(3 marks)**

# Fetch-decode-execute cycle 2

The registers, which are memory locations within the CPU, play an important role in the fetch-decode-execute cycle.

## How instructions are executed

This program instructs the CPU to carry out the calculation 6 + 13 and then to store the result.

| Program counter 0 | | | MAR 0 |
|---|---|---|---|
| MDR | LOAD 3 | The instruction at address 0 is fetched to the MDR. It is decoded to mean 'fetch the data from address 3 and put it in the accumulator'. | |
| Accumulator | 13 | 13 is stored in the accumulator. | |

| RAM | |
|---|---|
| Address | Contents |
| 0 | , LOAD 3 |
| 1 | ADD 4 |
| 2 | STORE 5 |
| 3 | 13 |
| 4 | 6 |
| 5 | |

| Program counter 1 | | | MAR 1 |
|---|---|---|---|
| MDR | ADD 4 | The instruction at address 1 is fetched to the MDR. It is decoded to mean 'fetch the data from address 4 and add to the value in the accumulator'. | |
| Accumulator | 19 | 6 is added to the accumulator to give a total of 19. | |

| RAM | |
|---|---|
| Address | Contents |
| 0 | LOAD 3 |
| 1 | , ADD 4 |
| 2 | STORE 5 |
| 3 | 13 |
| 4 | 6 |
| 5 | |

| Program counter 2 | | | MAR 2 |
|---|---|---|---|
| MDR | STORE 5 | The instruction at address 2 is fetched to the MDR. It is decoded to mean 'store the value in the accumulator in memory address 5'. | |
| Accumulator | 19 | 19 is stored in memory address 5. | |

| RAM | |
|---|---|
| Address | Contents |
| 0 | LOAD 3 |
| 1 | ADD 4 |
| 2 | , STORE 5 |
| 3 | 13 |
| 4 | 6 |
| 5 | 19 |

## Worked example

State the role of the following registers in the fetch-decode-execute cycle.

The question asks you to **state** and therefore a long explanation or description is **not** required. The statements should just state the role and not go into detail about how the roles are carried out.

• The program counter. **(1 mark)**

The program counter holds the memory address of the next instruction to be processed.

• The memory data register (MDR). **(1 mark)**

The memory data register holds an instruction or data that has been fetched from the memory before it is used.

## Now try this

State the role of these registers in the fetch-decode-execute cycle.

• The memory address register (MAR).

• The accumulator. **(2 marks)**

# Performance of the CPU

The speed at which the CPU processes program instructions can be increased by improving its design and adding components.

## Clock speed

The clock is a vibrating quartz crystal and the **faster it vibrates, the faster the instructions are processed** – at least 1 per cycle. Rates of 3GHz are common in modern computers.

The processor **generates a lot of heat** and the amount increases with the rate at which it processes instructions. The faster the clock speed, the hotter it gets, which causes it to malfunction and therefore it cannot be increased indefinitely.

The processor must have a **heat sink** and a fan to dissipate this heat. Liquid nitrogen is needed to cool supercomputers with clock speeds of 9GHz.

## Cache memory

☑ Cache memory is **very fast memory**, usually within the processor itself.

☑ The cache speeds up processing by **storing recently or frequently used instructions** so that they do not have to be fetched from the main memory which is much slower.

☑ As the cache becomes larger it takes longer to find the data and so it becomes slower. Therefore, it is split into different levels, e.g. L1, L2 with the smallest nearest to the CPU.

☑ Cache memory is far too expensive to use for the main memory (RAM) in personal computers.

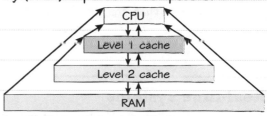

## Multi-core processors

A **multi-core processor** contains more than one CPU. Multi-core processors can give faster processing speeds than single-core processors, and can work on different tasks at the same time.

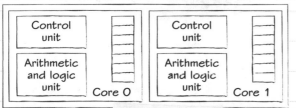

A multi-core processor with two cores - a dual-core processor.

## Using multi-core processors

👍 The cores can work together on the same program – *parallel processing*.

👍 The cores can work on different programs at the same time – *multitasking*.

👎 Not all programs will run at twice the speed with a dual-core processor.

👎 The programs may be sequential so that one task requires output from a previous task and so the second task cannot start until the first has finished.

Explain why the cache size affects the performance of the CPU. **(4 marks)**

Cache is high speed memory used to store frequently used program instructions. The larger the cache size, the less often the slower main memory needs to be accessed, speeding up data transfer. The performance of the CPU will be improved as it does not have to wait as long for the data to be delivered. However, if the cache becomes too large then the data access time increases and so the cache is split into units e.g. L1, L2, L3.

The question uses the word **explain** so you should give a detailed account stating that it is faster to transfer data and where data is transferred from and to.

Explain why increasing the number of cores in a processor does not necessarily increase the rate at which all programs are processed. **(2 marks)**

# Embedded systems

An embedded system is a computer system built into another device in order to control it.

## Components in embedded systems

Components in embedded systems are on a single printed circuit board (PCB). They include the:

- processor
- memory
- input and output interfaces.

Input devices may be manual switches and dials, such as on washing machines. The input interfaces must convert changes in them into electrical signals. A PCB is the base that supports the components that are soldered to it or fitted into sockets.

## Tasks

Each embedded system is **built for a small range of specific tasks** unlike desktop and laptop computers that are general purpose and are capable of carrying out many different tasks.

Washing machine

Digital camera

### Real-time systems

Embedded systems are called **real-time systems** because they must ensure an immediate response in order for the system to react to different situations, e.g. when the button is pressed on a camera or when the brakes are applied in a car.

**These devices all have embedded systems to control their functions**

Microwave oven

---

## Worked example

Many modern devices use embedded systems to function properly.

Explain **one** function of an embedded system in a washing machine. **(2 marks)**

It monitors the water temperature so that it can turn the heating element on and off to maintain the correct temperature.

The question uses the word **explain** so you need to give a function **and** the reason why the function is needed.
You could also have answered that the embedded system monitors the spin speed setting so that it sets the motor to the correct speed.

---

## Now try this

Many modern devices contain embedded systems.

 (a) Define the term 'embedded system'. **(1 mark)**

(b) Explain the role of embedded systems in real-time applications. **(2 marks)**

# RAM and ROM

RAM and ROM are two types of computer memory.

## RAM

**Random access memory (RAM)** is where the computer stores data and instructions when an application is running.

👍 Data can be read from and **written to** RAM.

👎 RAM is **volatile** – if you turn off the power, data in RAM is lost.

RAM is often removable. You can upgrade many computers by adding more RAM.

## ROM

**Read only memory (ROM)** is used to store instructions that don't need to be changed during normal use.

👎 Data can only be **read** from ROM.

👍 ROM is **non-volatile** – it retains data even if the power is turned off.

In a PC, the sets of instructions needed for the computer to start up are stored in ROM. These instructions need to be stored and saved even after the power is turned off.

## How much RAM?

Some applications (such as photo- or video-editing) require greater amounts of RAM. Here are four common devices with typical amounts of RAM.

Smartphone: 2GB

Games console: 4GB

Laptop: 8GB

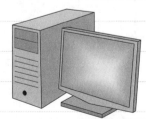

Workstation: 16GB or more

(a) Describe the role of programs stored in ROM.    **(2 marks)**

Programs stored in ROM carry out specific tasks including initialising hardware components and starting the operating system when a computer is switched on.

(b) Describe the difference between volatile and non-volatile memory.    **(2 marks)**

The content of non-volatile memory is not lost when the power is turned off whereas the content of volatile memory is erased. The content of volatile memory changes constantly whereas the content of non-volatile memory is fixed and cannot be altered.

Questions like this require both elements to be addressed in the description in order to be awarded the marks.

 1 State which type of memory is used to store application data during execution.    **(1 mark)**

 2 Give **two** differences between RAM and ROM.    **(2 marks)**

# Virtual memory

Virtual memory is an area of the hard disc drive or solid-state drive used as temporary RAM when the actual RAM is full.

## Use of virtual memory

Program instructions and data are constantly moving between the CPU and the RAM.

RAM may become full if many programs are running.

CPU

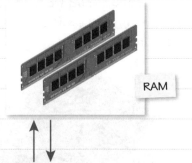

RAM

If there is no free RAM, the operating system (OS) will **swap out** some of the data stored in RAM to the **virtual memory** on the hard disc drive and swap in the requested data into the free area of the RAM.

Hard disc drive

## Swapping data

Usually the **least recently used** stored data is swapped out. If data is swapped out and is then needed again, it is swapped back in from the virtual memory at the expense of other data. The more RAM a computer has then the less virtual memory will be needed. Adding more RAM will **significantly improve the performance** of a computer.

> Make sure you include both **how** and **why** it is used.

## Disadvantages of using virtual memory

- 💭 The read/write speed of a magnetic hard drive is much **slower than RAM**. There will be a significant performance drop if the system has to rely too heavily on virtual memory.
- 💭 If the OS is constantly swapping between RAM and the hard disc drive, programs will run more slowly. This is called **disc thrashing**.

## Worked example

A computer's operating system uses 6 GB of virtual memory.

(a) Explain how a computer uses virtual memory and why it may be necessary. **(2 marks)**

A computer uses virtual memory by moving to it the least recently used instructions and data from main memory. This allows other data to be loaded into the main memory. A computer uses virtual memory to compensate for not having a sufficient amount of RAM.

(b) State **one** advantage and **one** disadvantage of the use of virtual memory. **(2 marks)**

An advantage of virtual memory is that program operation will continue even when the main memory is full.

A disadvantage of virtual memory is that there is a fall in performance as it is much slower to access the data.

### Now try this

Explain why adding more RAM to a computer will improve its performance. **(2 marks)**

# Secondary storage 1: optical and magnetic devices

Data can be stored on secondary storage devices. There are three main types of storage device: magnetic discs, optical discs and solid-state (flash) memory.

For more on solid state (flash) memory, see page 10.

## The need for secondary storage

Data and programs are stored **permanently** on secondary storage devices but the CPU cannot access them directly and so they must be transferred to (loaded into) the main memory.

Secondary storage devices can also be used to transfer stored data between computers.

## Magnetic storage

Magnetic storage is used in hard disc drives (HDDs) and digital tape drives which are often used for backing up large computer systems. **Magnetic discs** consist of stacks of non-removable discs coated with magnetic materials.

Hard disc drive

Data is encoded as opposing magnetic polarities on the surface of the disc. Electromagnets in the read/write heads read and write the data.

The cost of magnetic storage is very low. Hard disc drives in budget laptops have capacities of at least 1 terabyte.

Digital tape drive

## Worked example

A small business backs up the data on its computer system every day.

Compare backing up the data to a magnetic hard disc with backing up to an optical disc. **(4 marks)**

Data is written to and read from a magnetic hard disc more quickly than to/from an optical disc, so backing up and restoring would be quicker.

Hard discs are permanently located within a hard disc drive so are less portable than optical discs, such as DVDs, which can be removed from the drive when not in use. Portable hard drives are very light and compact so could be stored off-site. Optical media tends to be more durable than magnetic media. DVDs offer unlimited storage because the business can use as many as needed. HDDs can store several terabytes of data which would probably be enough for the business.

For more on the features of secondary storage, see page 11.

## Optical storage

Optical storage includes:

- compact discs (CDs) that store 700MB
- digital versatile discs (DVDs) that store 4.7GB
- Blu-ray discs that store up to 50GB.

Optical discs use a laser to read and write data. The data is encoded as a series of pits in a spiral track running from the inside to the outside of the disc.

CD, DVD and Blu-ray drives write and read data onto discs using light from lasers.

## Now try this

Explain why secondary storage devices are needed. **(3 marks)**

# Secondary storage 2: solid-state memory

Unlike magnetic and optical storage devices there are no moving parts in solid-state devices.

## Solid-state memory

Solid-state memory is made of **flash memory**. Flash memory is **non-volatile** storage that can be electrically erased and reprogrammed. Flash memory uses arrays of transistors (switches). Transistors can operate in two states, 0 and 1, and are switched from one to the other using electrical signals. Data is encoded as sets of binary digits. 8 GB of solid-state storage require 32 billion transistors.

> The question asks you to **explain**. Don't just state 'they use electricity, magnetism and light'.

## Worked example

Explain how each of these secondary storage devices physically records data.

• Magnetic hard drive.
• Flash memory USB stick.
• Optical disc drive.                    **(3 marks)**

Hard disc drives use electromagnetism to store data magnetically on metal discs.

Data is stored in flash memory by using electricity to change the state of the transistors it is made of.

DVDs use light produced by a laser to store data on the disc by changing its surface.

## Uses of solid-state memory

Solid-state memory is used for data storage in portable devices such as cameras and mobile phones.

| Solid-state drives (SSDs) | | Solid-state drives (SSDs) can provide secondary storage instead of magnetic discs. |
|---|---|---|
| Secure digital (SD) cards | | Secure digital (SD) cards and microSD cards are used in portable devices such as phones, cameras and tablets. |
| USB flash drives | | USB flash drives are convenient compact forms of flash memory for sharing and transferring data. |

## Now try this

1  List **two** advantages of using a flash memory device rather than a magnetic hard disc drive for data storage.                    **(2 marks)**

2  State **one** disadvantage of using flash memory.                    **(1 mark)**

# Storage 3: capacity, speed and cost

The different storage devices have different properties.

## Comparison of secondary storage devices

| Type of storage | Capacity | Speed | Cost |
|---|---|---|---|
| Magnetic | Very large<br>1–2 TB is common in home computers.<br>Can store 1000 to 2000 movies (assuming an average size of 1GB). | Fast<br>Random access: data can be read instantly from any part of the disc.<br>Can find and supply required data in milliseconds (thousands of a second). | Very low<br>Magnetic drives storing terabytes of data are common in most home computers. |
| Optical | Low<br>CDs store 700MB<br>DVDs store 4.7 GB<br>Can store four movies. | Slow | Very low |
| Solid state | Moderate<br>Solid state drives are usually from 128–512 GB but the capacity is rapidly increasing.<br>Can store up to 500 movies. | Very fast<br>Can access data in nanoseconds (thousands of a millisecond). | More expensive than magnetic drives and optical devices.<br>Solid state storage is a relatively young technology. Storage capacity is rapidly increasing and the cost is falling. |

☐ good    ☐ moderate    ▨ poor

---

### Worked example

A school has a number of different data storage requirements.

State which type of secondary storage is most suitable for each of the purposes listed below. Give a reason for your choice.

- Hand-held data-logging devices used for fieldwork.

Solid state. Very fast access speed for taking readings and not sensitive to being moved around.

- Storage drives on the school's file server to save all of the students' work.

Magnetic. Very large capacity, reliable and low cost.

- Copies of a video of a school production to be given to parents. **(6 marks)**

Optical. Discs are cheap and portable and most home computers can access them.

> Make sure you state an appropriate type of storage and suggest a reason. If you can easily think of more than one reason then you could write them down, just to be sure.

### Now try this

Explain why nowadays many laptops and desktop computers have built-in solid-state drives rather than hard disc drives.

**(3 marks)**

# Storage 4: portability, durability and reliability

The different secondary storage devices each have benefits and drawbacks depending on the situation.

## Comparison of secondary storage devices

| Type of storage | Portability | Durability | Reliability |
|---|---|---|---|
| Magnetic | Not very portable as physical knocks may cause the read/write heads to hit the discs and corrupt data. | Very durable. | Very reliable. |
| Optical | More portable than a hard disc drive but discs are relatively large. | Easily scratched and data can be corrupted. Data cannot be overwritten. Stored data degrade over time. | Very reliable if they are not scratched. |
| Solid state | Very portable. Small solid-state storage devices can be fitted inside cameras and mobile phones. | Limited number of erase/write cycles. | Very reliable and data are not affected by magnetic fields (as they are in magnetic drives). |

☐ good  ☐ moderate  ☐ poor

## Worked example

Anna is buying a new laptop computer. She has the choice between a magnetic hard disc drive and a SSD for file storage.

Discuss the benefits and drawbacks of these alternative secondary storage devices. **(6 marks)**

At present, the storage capacity of hard disc drives is greater than for SSDs so Anna would be able to store more files.

Also, at present, the cost of hard disc drive storage is cheaper than for SSDs although the cost is falling.

SSD data access speeds are far greater than for hard disc drives.

SSDs have no moving parts so they are ideal for laptops as they will not be damaged if they are dropped.

As data becomes fragmented, access is slower on hard disc drives as the read/write heads have to move to different platters to access different parts of the same file. Fragmentation does not slow data access in SSDs as there are no moving read/write heads.

The two methods, hard disc drives and SSDs, have to be compared and each point should mention both.
Just saying that 'SSDs are fast at accessing data' would not answer the question as the answer is not comparing the SSD with a hard disc drive.

## Now try this

Identify **four** factors, other than cost, that should be considered when choosing a secondary storage device. **(4 marks)**

# Networks 1: LANs and WANs

A computer network is a group of computer systems and other devices linked together so that they can communicate and share resources such as printers. Networks can be as small as two computers and a printer in a home network.

## Local area network (LAN)

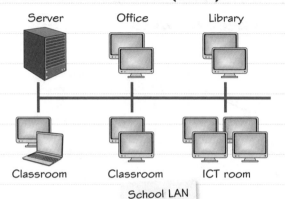

Server   Office   Library

Classroom   Classroom   ICT room

School LAN

A **local area network** is a network in a small area such as a home, school, office building or group of buildings on a single site. It exists within a small geographical area. A LAN is usually managed by a local manager or team at the site. Many people have a home LAN that allows the members of a household to access the internet using a wireless router.

The internet is a global system of interconnected computer networks. Hyperlinks can take you from a host computer in one LAN to a computer in another. The internet is therefore an example of a huge WAN.

See page 17 for more about the internet.

## Wide area network (WAN)

**Wide area networks** connect separate LANs over a large geographical area to form a network of networks. Large companies can connect LANs at their different sites in order to share resources and data. Computers in a WAN can communicate with computers and users in other locations.

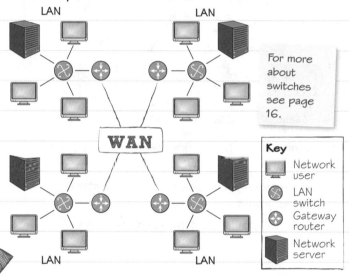

LAN   LAN

WAN

LAN   LAN

For more about switches see page 16.

Key
🖥 Network user
✕ LAN switch
✷ Gateway router
▨ Network server

The WAN will be managed by several different people or parts of an organisation working together (collective ownership). Alternatively, each LAN could be managed independently (distributed ownership).

### Factors affecting network performance

☑ **Bandwidth** is the maximum amount of data that can pass through the medium per second.

☑ **Hardware** and **software** limitations (switches and routers) can affect performance.

☑ A high **number of users** can cause network congestion, leading to packets being queued before they can be transmitted by routers and switches.

☑ **High network traffic** can lead to collisions of data packets resulting in transmission errors. The packets have to be resent.

## Worked example

State **one** way in which a local area network (LAN) and a wide area network (WAN).

**(1 mark)**

A LAN is a network that is restricted to one building or site.

A WAN is a network of separate LANs over a large geographical area.

## Now try this

A retailer wants to share data between its head office and its 300 high street stores.
Explain why the business would use a WAN rather than a LAN for this purpose.

**(2 marks)**

# Networks 2: client–server and peer-to-peer

Computer networks can range from small networks on a single site to much larger networks operating across continents and there are different types to cater for the needs of both.

## Client–server network

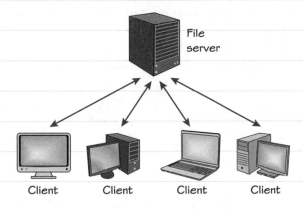

File server

Client   Client   Client   Client

## Peer-to-peer network

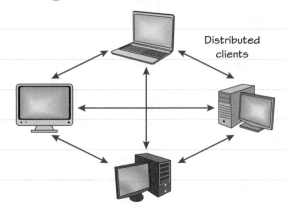

Distributed clients

In client–server networks there are two types of computer:

- **file servers** – computers which control access and manage the network
- **clients** – computers on which the users work.

In peer-to-peer networks, there is only one type of computer.

- There is **no server** to manage the network. All the computers are connected together equally.
- They are **all equal** and can communicate with each other directly without having to go through a server.

## Using a client–server network

- Users **log in** to the servers to access programs and data stored on them.
- Servers are responsible for network security by allocating login names and passwords to users.
- All files are held on the servers and can be backed up centrally.

## Using a peer-to-peer network

- Each client can act as a server. Other clients can share programs, data, and printers.
- Security is distributed – each user can grant rights to others and allocate passwords.
- Data is stored on each client and not centrally.
- Each user is responsible for backing up each client.

## Worked example

List **three** benefits of using a client–server rather than a peer-to-peer network.  **(3 marks)**

Network security is controlled centrally rather than on each client.
All files can be saved centrally rather than on each client.
All backups can be done centrally rather than having to be done on each client.

The question asks you to **compare** the two types of network system by listing the benefits and drawbacks of one system over the other. You cannot just list the properties of a peer-to-peer network. You must show how these are benefits and drawbacks when compared with a client–server network.

## Now try this

List **three** benefits and **three** drawbacks of using a peer-to-peer network rather than a client–server network.  **(3 marks)**

# Transmission media

Devices on a network communicate through cables (wired) or by radio waves (wireless).

## Cable (wired)

Devices are physically connected using either **copper wire** or **fibre optic cable**.

| Copper wire | Fibre optic cable |
|---|---|
| Transmits data as electric signals. | Transmits data as pulses of light. |
| 👍 Cheaper than fibre optic. | 👍 Transmit signals at faster speeds and over greater distances than copper wire. |

## Bandwidth

Bandwidth is the amount of data that can be transmitted per second. Bandwidth is measured in bits per second (bps).

- Copper cable: up to 1 Gbps.
- Fibre optic: up to 10 Gbps.
- Wireless: up to 600 Mbps.

## Radio waves (wireless)

Wireless networks use radio waves, which are part of the electromagnetic spectrum, to communicate. The most commonly used frequencies for data transmission in wireless networks are 2.4 GHz and 5 GHz. (1 GHz = $10^9$ cycles per second.) The frequency range is divided into 14 channels spaced 5 MHz apart. Users can change the operating channel of their Wi-Fi device to prevent interference.

## Protocols and security

Protocols are the rules that computers must follow when communicating over a network.

- Ethernet protocols are used in cable networks.
- Wi-Fi protocols are used in wireless networks. Wi-Fi is one wireless technology that uses radio waves.
- Other wireless protocols include Bluetooth, 3G, 4G and Wi-Fi Direct.

There are no physical connections in Wi-Fi networks, so networks must be protected by encryption algorithms. The most commonly used are Wired Equivalent Privacy (WEP) and Wi-Fi Protected Access (WPA).

## Cable and wireless networks

| | Cable | Wireless |
|---|---|---|
| **Bandwidth** | High – up to 10 Gbps | Low – up to 600 Mbps |
| **Installation** | Difficult – must run cables throughout the site. | Easy – just need wireless access points. |
| **Cost** | Expensive – cost of cables and installation. | Cheap – just cost of wireless access points. |
| **Security** | Good – need to plug computer into a socket. | Poor – anyone within range can access the network. Must use security passwords. |
| **Interference** | Good – there is no interference with cables. | Not so good – signals can be affected by walls and other electronic equipment. |
| **Mobility** | Poor – need to plug computer into a socket. | Good – access can be from anywhere within range. |

**Worked example**

The question asks you to **state** and so simple statements are required without explanations.

(a) State **two** types of cable that can be used to network computers. **(2 marks)**

Copper wire and fibre optic cable.

(b) State **one** other transmission medium that can be used to connect computers together to form a network. **(1 mark)**

Microwaves or radio waves.

**Now try this**

A school is considering whether to install a cable or wireless network.

Explain **three** benefits of each type of network when used in a school situation. **(6 marks)**

# Connecting computers to a LAN

Hardware is required to connect all computers in a local area network (LAN).

## Network interface controller

Computers need a **network interface controller (NIC)** (or **adapter**) to connect to a network. The NIC formats the data sent to and received by the computer. NICs are often built on chips on the computer motherboard.

## MAC address

Every NIC is created with its own unique **media access control (MAC)** number programmed into it. The MAC address ensures that data is directed to the correct computer.

## Hub or switch?

- ✓ Hubs and switches are used to link computers so that they can communicate with each other once they have connected to the network using the NIC.
- ✓ **Hubs** send every message to every computer on the network. This creates extra unnecessary network traffic.
- ✓ **Switches** read the destination addresses (the MAC addresses of the computers to which the message is being sent) of the messages and relay them only to the intended recipients.
- ✓ Switches and hubs affect the performance of networks by their effect on the amount of network traffic.

## Routers

- ✓ Routers connect different networks together.
- ✓ They read address information and forward the messages to the correct network.
- ✓ Routers are used to transfer data between a home network and the internet.

## Wireless access points

- ✓ Wireless devices need wireless access points to connect to cabled networks.
- ✓ They convert data received through cables into wireless signals and vice versa.
- ✓ Like hubs, they do not read the destination addresses and direct messages to all devices.
- ✓ Wireless access points are often used for hotspots in public buildings.

How the router, switch / hub and access point connect to the hardware.

Internet — Router — Switch — Access Point — Computer — Computer — Laptop

Both hubs and switches can be used to connect the devices in a network.

(a) Explain **one** advantage of using a switch rather than a hub. **(2 marks)**

A switch reads the address information of each message and directs it to the correct recipient. This reduces the amount of network traffic whereas a hub sends a message to every computer, creating extra network traffic.

(b) State the function of a network router. **(1 mark)**

A router forwards data traffic between computer networks.

In part (a) be careful not to confuse a switch with a router. A router connects different networks together.

Part (b) uses the word **state**, so a statement about its function is needed. Stating 'it transmits messages from one network to another' would also have been a correct response.

Explain how a network switch is able to identify the correct computer to which it must transmit a message. **(2 marks)**

# The internet

The internet is a wide area network (WAN) – a huge network of networks with the computers linked by a combination of wired and wireless transmission media.

## Hosting

A **host** is a computer accessed by users at remote locations over networks, including the internet.

Web hosting companies rent space on their servers for websites. The hosting companies handle all of the technical and security issues.

## Domain names

Every computer using the internet has a unique **internet protocol (IP)** address so that the other computers know where to send any requested data such as web pages. The IP address is used on the internet in the same way as the MAC address is used on the LAN. IP addresses are either 32 bit (IPv4) or 128 bit (IPv6) numbers.

IP addresses are represented as URLs, e.g. www.mysite.co.uk as they are easier to remember mysite.co.uk is the **domain name**.

When a user uses the domain name, a **domain name service (DNS)** translates it back into the IP address.

## Domain name service (DNS)

When a browser requests access to a host using its domain name, the client computer contacts a DNS server. The DNS server contains a database of domain names that allows it to look up the domain name and return the IP address. This is known as **resolving the domain name**.

**①** A user enters the domain name into the browser on the client computer.

**⑥** The client then contacts the host using the IP address.

**②** The client contacts a DNS server to resolve the domain name.

**⑤** The server returns the IP address to the client.

**③** If the domain name is not in the server's database, it contacts another server.

**④** The second server resolves the domain name and returns it to the first server.

## Worked example

(a) Define what is meant by web hosting. **(2 marks)**

A web host provides space for a website on a server so that it can be accessed by internet users.

(b) Give **two** advantages of using a web host. **(2 marks)**

The user does not need the technical knowledge to set up a web server or ensure that it is secure from hackers.

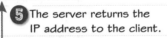

Part (a) asks you to **define**. Two points are required and the answer explains that space is provided on a server and that it allows access to internet users.

Part (b) asks you to **give** and full explanations are not required. Other correct answers could be that the user does not need to keep their computer switched on all the time or does not need to have a very high speed broadband connection.

## Now try this

1 Explain why domain names are used. **(2 marks)**

2 Describe the process that takes place when a user requests access to a host using its domain name.

**(3 marks)**

# Network topologies

The topology of a network describes how the devices are arranged and connected together.

## Star topology

In a star network, each computer or client is connected **individually** to a central point or **node**, which can be a file server, hub or switch.

Star network topology

For more about hubs and switches, see page 16.

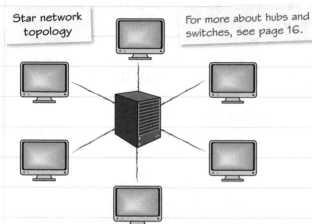

## Mesh topology

In a mesh network, each computer or client is connected to **all the other computers** in the network. Every computer sends its own signals but also relays data from the others. Mesh networks are commonly used with wireless networks where there is high demand.

Mesh network topology

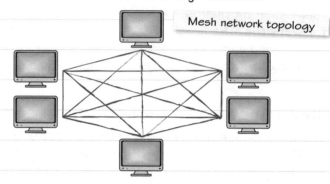

## Using a star network

👍 Data is only directed to the intended computer directly.

👍 Network traffic is kept to a minimum.

👍 If one link fails, all the other devices will continue to operate.

👍 It is easy to add new devices without disrupting the network.

👎 If the central point fails, then so will the entire network.

👎 Requires a lot of cable as each computer is connected individually to the central component.

## Using a mesh network

👍 Data can be transmitted from different devices simultaneously.

👍 If one component fails, there is always an alternative route for data.

👍 Can handle high volumes of data traffic.

👍 Adding more devices will not slow the data transmission.

👎 Overall cost is high. More cable is required unless a wireless network is used.

👎 Difficult to manage and requires expert supervision.

## Worked example

A small business has set up a network with a star topology.

Give **three** reasons why the business might choose a star topology for its LAN.  **(3 marks)**

It is easy to add new devices without disrupting the network.

Data can be sent only to the intended recipient without having to send it to all computers, which increases the efficiency of the network as there will be less network traffic.

If one computer fails it does not affect the rest of the network and the work of the business will be able to continue.

You must give **three** different reasons and a statement about each, this student has only given three. You could make comparisons with other topologies that highlight the advantages.

You do not need to spend time drawing accurate diagrams of computers. Simple boxes labelled 'computer' will be enough.

## Now try this

1 State what is meant by the term 'network topology'.  **(1 mark)**

2 With the aid of a diagram, describe a mesh network topology.  **(3 marks)**

3 Explain **one** advantage of a mesh network over a star network.  **(2 marks)**

# Protocols 1: browsers and email clients

Protocols are the rules that computers must follow when they are communicating and sending and receiving data over a network.

## Protocols

Protocols are needed to ensure that data is sent and received accurately, and that it is sent to the correct address on a network. Protocols need to include:

- data formats, to ensure that data can be exchanged consistently and correctly
- address formats, to identify senders and recipients and to ensure that data goes to the right places
- routing, to provide the right information so that data can flow through networks correctly.

## TCP/IP

TCP/IP stands for **T**ransmission **C**ontrol **P**rotocol/**I**nternet **P**rotocol. TCP/IP is a set or **stack** of protocols that allows a computer to communicate across a wide area network. The protocols:

- split the data into smaller **packets**, reassemble packets on arrival and encrypt/ decrypt as required
- add an address in order to transmit the data to the correct destination
- notify the sending computer that the data has been received.

For more about TCP/IP, see page 20.

## Protocols used by applications such as web browsers and email clients

| | |
|---|---|
| FTP | **File Transfer Protocol** provides the rules for file transfer between computers. It is often used to transfer files that are too large for attachment to emails. |
| HTTP | **Hypertext Transfer Protocol** provides the rules to be followed by a web browser and a web server when requesting and supplying information. It is used for sending requests from a web client (a browser) to a web server and returning web content from the server back to the client. |
| HTTPS | **Secure HTTP** ensures that communications between a host and client are secure by encrypting communications. |
| SMTP | **Simple Mail Transfer Protocol** provides the rules for sending email messages from client to server and then from server to server until it reaches its destination. |
| POP | **Post Office Protocol** is used by a client to retrieve emails from a mail server. All of the emails are downloaded when there is a connection between client and server. |
| IMAP | **Internet Message Access Protocol.** Unlike POP, the messages do not have to be downloaded. They can be read and stored on the message server. This is better for users with many different devices as they can be read from all devices rather than being downloaded to just one. |

## Worked example

TCP/IP is a protocol stack used to transmit data over a wide area network.

List **three** tasks carried out by protocols in the transmission of data over a network.    **(3 marks)**

Split the data into packets.

Add the address of the recipient computer.

Notify the sending computer when the data is received.

## Now try this

POP and IMAP are both email protocols. Explain how they differ from each other and give a benefit of each.    **(3 marks)**

This is a **list** question, so it does not need any descriptions or explanations.

# Protocols 2: network layers

Protocols are organised into separate layers of the four layer TCP/IP suite. It is sometimes called a 'stack' as the protocols are organised in four levels.

## Network layers

The protocols of the TCP/IP stack are organised into layers through which all data must pass. Incoming and outgoing data pass through the layers where packaging data are added or read.

## The four layer TCP/IP model

Each layer of the model has a specific job to do in order for communication to take place over the network.

| Purpose | Layer | Protocols |
|---------|-------|-----------|
| Provides services to applications such as web browsers and email clients. This is where requests are made to web servers or emails are sent. | Application layer | FTP, HTTP, HTTPS, SMTP, POP, IMAP<br><br>See page 19 for more on these protocols. |
| Divides data sent from the application layer into packets. Checks that data sent has been received and notifies sender that data has been received. | Transport layer | Transmission Control Protocol (TCP)<br>User Datagram Protocol (UDP) |
| Adds the source and destination IP addresses to the data and routes it to the recipient computer. | Internet layer (also called Network layer) | Internet Protocol (IP) |
| Uses network-specific protocols to ensure correct transmission of data through the local network. | Network Access layer (also called Data Link layer) | Ethernet or Wi-Fi Protocols |

## Worked example

TCP/IP is a protocol stack used in networking. Place the four layers of the TCP/IP stack into order (1–4, where 1 is the top layer and 4 is the bottom layer). **(2 marks)**

| Layer | Order (1–4) |
|-------|-------------|
| Transport | 2 |
| Network Access | 4 |
| Internet | 3 |
| Application | 1 |

This question does not require any descriptions or explanations.

The question must be read carefully to ensure that you know whether 1 represents the top or the bottom layer.

Mnemonics are a good way of remembering things and the following one helps with remembering the order of the layers:

TCP/IP comes in A TIN.

## Now try this

TCP/IP is a protocol stack used in networking.

Explain what is meant by the term 'protocol stack'.

**(3 marks)**

# Protocol 3: benefits of layers

There are advantages to organising the protocols into the separate layers of the four layer TCP/IP model.

## Benefits of organising protocols into layers

Each layer in the TCP/IP model contains specific hardware and software to perform particular tasks.

👍 The overall model is simplified by dividing it into functional parts.

👍 Different layers can be combined in different ways as required.

👍 One layer can be developed or changed without affecting the other layers.

👍 Allocating specific tasks makes it easier to identify and correct networking errors and problems.

👍 It provides a universal standard for hardware and software manufacturers to follow so that their devices will be able to communicate with each other.

## Virtual networks

Virtual networking allows users to communicate locally and remotely across similar and dissimilar networks through a simple and consistent user interface.

👍 Users can access resources anywhere around the world as though they are on a local network.

👍 Virtual networking makes it possible to interact with a computer from any other computer or mobile device on the internet.

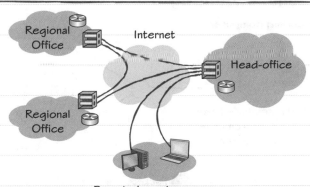

Remote/roaming users

A virtual private network (VPN) allows users to communicate securely using an internet connection. Data that are sent are placed within an outer packet that only that particular VPN can understand using special protocols.

## Worked example

State which protocol is used in these situations:

• to transfer files between computers

FTP

• to make a secure payment

HTTPS

• to send an email. **(3 marks)**

SMTP

In this question, only the protocols should be stated and no explanation or description is required.

## Now try this

Describe **three** advantages of organising TCP/IP protocols into layers. **(6 marks)**

# Packets and packet switching

Data must be transferred between computers as securely and efficiently as possible. This is especially important as more data is being stored in the cloud.

## Packets

When data is transferred between computers, (e.g. via email or uploading to cloud storage), it is split into **packets** to avoid the high bandwidth needed for large files.

Each packet consists of a:

- header containing the source and destination addresses and the position of the packet in the complete message
- body containing some of the data
- footer to inform the receiving device that this is the end of the packet.

## The cloud

**Cloud storage** is off-site storage accessed via the internet. Data can be stored and accessed on remote servers in vast data centres around the world.

👍 Data can be accessed from anywhere and many users can share the data.

👎 The hosting company could be targeted by hackers.

👎 Download and upload speed might be low.

## Packet switching

Sending computer                                   Receiving computer

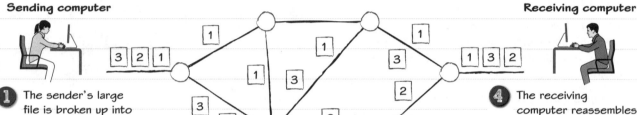

① The sender's large file is broken up into smaller packets.

Key
○ Routers

② Packets are directed to their destination by routers. Routers inspect the packets and decide the most efficient path to the next router.

③ Packets take different routes across the network. They may not arrive in the correct order.

④ The receiving computer reassembles them in the correct order using information in the headers.

(a) Explain what is meant by a packet switching network. **(2 marks)**

In a packet switching network there is no dedicated line between the source and recipient computers as there would be for a land-line telephone call. The data is divided into packets and reassembled in the correct order when they reach their destination. Data packets can take different routes to their destination.

(b) State **one** benefit of a packet switching network. **(1 mark)**

If there is a problem or congestion in one part of the network, then the packets can be sent by a different route to avoid it.

In part (a) the word **explain** is used and therefore a simple statement is not enough. The answer makes two points – that there is no dedicated line **and** that data packets can take different routes.

In part (b) a 'benefit' has been stated. Just saying 'the packets can be sent by different routes' would not state the 'benefit' without mentioning congestion or problems on the network.

Discuss the advantages and disadvantages of using cloud storage. **(6 marks)**

# Threats to networks 1: people as the weak point

There are many ways in which networks can be attacked. Many target the people who use them.

## Targeting the users – social engineering

Social engineering involves tricking people into divulging secret information such as passwords and login information.

**Phishing** involves emails claiming or appearing to be from a bank or building society e-commerce site, asking for details of passwords and credit cards.

**Blagging** involves a criminal inventing a scenario to persuade a victim to give out information, e.g. they could pretend to be another employee or a network administrator.

**Social engineering**

**Shouldering** involves finding passwords and PINs (Personal Identification Numbers) by watching people enter them. This could happen in a busy office or at a distance using binoculars or recording equipment.

## Poor network policies

All organisations should have an **acceptable use policy** that all users must read, sign and abide by. It should include items concerned with security such as:

- Users must not use their own devices (such as USB flash drives) on the network. These devices pose a threat as malware can be introduced to the network and data can be removed and stolen.

- Users must not download files from the internet as these could be infected with malware.

## Password policy

**Weak passwords** are a major security risk. A weak password is one that can be easily and quickly guessed by humans and computers. Hackers often use brute-force techniques, employing software that tries every single combination of letters, numbers and symbols until it finds the correct combination.

- A long password with a combination of letters, numbers and symbols will take longer to guess.
- Passwords should be changed regularly and old ones should never be reused.
- Hackers can also find out users' details such as their dates of birth or names of relatives and these should never be used in passwords.

## Worked example

Describe **two** different types of threat to a company's network security posed by its own employees.

**(4 marks)**

Employees are subject to social engineering where criminals try to find security information by activities such as phishing, shouldering and blagging.

Employees may also install malware such as viruses, worms, Trojans and adware onto the system when they are downloading files or answering emails.

The question asks for 'different types' and so just mentioning two examples of social engineering or two examples of malware would not have included different types of security threat.

## Now try this

1 Describe what is meant by the term 'social engineering'. **(2 marks)**

2 Describe **two** different social engineering techniques. **(4 marks)**

Had a look ☐  Nearly there ☐  Nailed it! ☐

# Threats to networks 2: malware

Many forms of attack target users by getting them to install malware (harmful software) on their computers.

## Malware

Malware is software that has been designed to gain unauthorised access to a computer system in order to disrupt its functioning, or collect information.

A **virus** is a computer program hidden inside another program. Viruses can delete or corrupt data held on an infected computer. A virus can replicate itself and insert itself into other programs or files that can then be passed on.

A **worm** does not need another program to carry it. It can replicate and send itself in emails that are then sent to everyone in a user's address book. Worms consume computer resources as they are reproducing and allow criminals to gain access to the infected computer and take it over.

### Types of malware

**Spyware** often comes packaged with other software and the user does not know they are installing it. It spies on the user like a Trojan by sending information to a criminal.

**Adware** displays unwanted adverts or diverts browser requests to advertising sites.

**Trojans** are installed by users when they think they are installing legitimate software.

Trojans can delete files, change the desktop layout and send screenshots and key presses to the hacker's computer.

## Preventing infection

- ✓ Install antivirus software and ensure that it is constantly updated.
- ✓ Ensure that the antivirus software can scan emails.
- ✓ Use adware removal software.
- ✓ Install anti-spyware protection software that removes or blocks spyware.
- ✓ Avoid opening emails and attachments from unknown sources.
- ✓ Install a firewall to ensure that software is not downloaded without your knowledge.
- ✓ Ensure that the operating system is up to date.
- ✓ Install the latest security updates.

### Worked example

Describe what is meant by 'malware'. **(2 marks)**

Malware is software that has been designed to gain unauthorised access to a computer system in order to disrupt its functioning or collect information.

The answer uses the less specific wording 'to disrupt its functioning'. Saying 'to corrupt or delete data' would not be correct as not all malware does that.

### Now try this

List **five** precautions that a user should take in order to minimise the risk of their computer being infected with malware.

**(5 marks)**

# Threats to networks 3: network security

Many attacks on networks use methods that bypass the users and target the network operating system and security.

```
socket, sys, os
][VIRUS DETECTED!!!"
injecting " + sys.arg
ack():
```
Malware detected in computer system.

**Brute-force attacks** are general attacks that need little special knowledge or techniques.
- Automated software is used to try millions of different passwords.
- Success is based on computing power rather than any specialist techniques.

**Data interception and theft** involves the use of packet analysers (packet sniffers) to intercept data packets on a network, which are then analysed. Sensitive data such as login names, passwords and credit card numbers can be stolen.

## Methods of attack

**Denials of service** overload a network or website by flooding it with network communications such as login requests.
- Malware can be used to take control of lots of computers (zombies) that will all send information and login requests at the same time. This is called a distributed denial of service (DDoS) attack.
- The attacks may be used to extort money or they may be organised by rival organisations.
- They are often used by hacktivists to punish organisations they think are unethical.

**SQL injection** exploits personal and financial data held on websites (such as social networking sites, banks and online commerce sites) stored in huge databases.
**SQL (structured query language)** is used to manipulate data, e.g. to create new records, search for information and check login names and passwords. Criminals can create commands entered in login fields to bypass security and gain access to records and steal valuable data such as names, addresses and bank details.

## Worked example

A hacker uses software that tries out millions of combinations of letters, numbers and symbols to attempt to find a user's password.

Explain why this is referred to as a brute-force attack.

**(2 marks)**

It is called brute force as no specialist techniques are used. Raw computing power is used to try millions of combinations.

Although a brute-force attack may be able to gain access to an account eventually, these attacks can take several hours, days, months and even years to run. The time to complete an attack depends on the password and the power of the computer(s) used to conduct the attack.

## Now try this

When the computers of a major online gaming company crashed they claimed that it was the result of a distributed denial of service attack (DDoS).

Explain what is meant by a DDoS.

**(4 marks)**

# Identifying and preventing vulnerabilities 1

All networks must be protected against unauthorised access by identifying risks and applying measures to prevent them.

## Penetration testing

Penetration testing is used to test a computer system or network in order to find vulnerabilities that an attacker could exploit.

- Testers take the role of hackers and try to gain unauthorised access.
- Testing also assesses the security awareness of users and demonstrates the effectiveness of network security policies.

## Network forensics

Network forensics is the monitoring, recording and analysis of network events such as:

- who has logged in
- how many unsuccessful attempts have been made
- what users have done
- what has been deleted.

Network forensics can identify unusual network activity. The analysis can be used as legal evidence if illegal activity is detected.

## User measures

**Passwords** should be:
- strong – at least eight characters and include non-alphanumeric characters, e.g. ! or ?
- changed regularly
- never written down or shared
- old passwords should never be reused.

**User access levels** are used to set which files and folders users are allowed to:
- see and browse
- edit or delete.

### User measures to prevent vulnerabilities

**Network policies** are rules that should set out:
- what users can and cannot do on the network, e.g. must not use removable storage devices, install their own software or download files from internet sites
- when backups will be made and where they will be kept
- what should be done if there is a problem or breach of security.

## Worked example

Network policies often restrict the use of removable media on the network.

(a) State **two** types of removable media that workers might use on their journey to and from work. **(2 marks)**

Smartphone, MP3 player, camera.

(b) State **two** reasons why the use of removable media on the network might be restricted. **(2 marks)**

Malware could be introduced to the network.
Data could be copied and stolen.

The question asks you to **state** and therefore extra details are not required.
The question asks for removable media that users are likely to be carrying with them on their journey into work. A removable hard disc drive would not fall into this category!

Workers who use removable media must abide by policies put in place to safeguard the business network.

## Now try this

List **three** rules that should be applied when creating a strong password. **(3 marks)**

# Identifying and preventing vulnerabilities 2

System measures can also be taken to protect networks from threats.

### 1 Anti-malware software

- This software is designed to detect and remove malware, e.g. antivirus or spyware removal software.
- Anti-malware software should be constantly updated to tackle new threats.
- Operating systems should be kept up to date as new security features are introduced.

### 2 Encryption

- Encryption is the conversion of data into a form that cannot be understood unless a user knows how to convert it back again.
- These conversions are called ENCRYPTING and DECRYPTING the data.
- A common method is to use a 'public' and 'private' key:
  - a user would encrypt a message to send using the recipient's public key that is available to all...
  - ...but only the recipient's private key is able to decrypt it.

### 3 Firewalls

- A firewall protects a network connected to a WAN such as the internet.
- It can be provided by hardware or software.
- Firewalls can be configured to prevent communications from entering the network and also to prevent programs and users from accessing the internet from within the network.

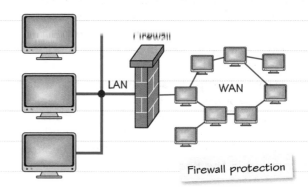

Firewall protection

## Worked example

 (a) Explain why data within a network should be encrypted. **(2 marks)**

If data is not encrypted, it can be read by anyone who has access to the file. Criminals can gain access online and steal data and laptops and portable hard disc drives can be lost or stolen.

> Part (a) asks you to **explain** and therefore a longer answer is expected.

 (b) Describe how messages sent between two users can be encrypted. **(4 marks)**

This can be done using a private and public key. A message to a user is encrypted using their public key that is available to all users. Only the intended recipient can decrypt it using their private key.

> Part (b) also expects a longer answer as you are being asked to **describe** how data can be encrypted.

## Now try this

Explain why all networks should be protected by a firewall. **(4 marks)**

# Operating systems 1

Systems software runs and maintains the computer system and manages user interactions with it. Systems software comprises the operating system and utility software.

## Systems software

The **operating system** of a computer:

- manages users' interactions through the user interface
- manages peripheral devices
- controls computing processes
- allocates CPU and memory resources.

**Utility software** on a computer is a set of tools that can be used to analyse and optimise efficiency.

## Application software

**Application software** is an **end-user program**. Also called **apps** or **applications**, end-user programs perform user-identified tasks such as word processing and photo editing or are used for entertainment, such as games and viewing videos.

Find out more about utility software on page 30.

## Memory management

In a computer system, many programs will be running at the same time. This is called **multitasking**. Although programs appear to run concurrently, the operating system is sharing out processor time between them so that, in turn, they can have their program instructions processed.

The activities the programs are performing are called **processes**. Some processes are visible to the user as application software, but many are not seen by the user. There are usually programs and processes that the user cannot see running in the background.

> All processes require the use of the CPU and memory.
>
> ⇩
>
> The operating system prioritises the tasks and allocates time to each process.
>
> ⇩
>
> It checks that all requests for memory are valid and allocates it accordingly.
>
> ⇩
>
> It also swaps out data to the virtual memory when the main memory is full.

Find out about virtual memory on page 8.

## Worked example

Explain the purpose of an operating system.

**(4 marks)**

The operating system provides an interface between the hardware, software and users and so allows the computer users to load and run programs, create and save documents, etc.

It is responsible for memory management as different programs will be requesting the loading of instructions and data.

It allocates CPU time to the different applications as they all require the CPU to execute the program instructions.

It manages the input and output devices required for the input and output of data.

## File management

The operating system creates a folder and file structure for data. This makes it easier for users to organise and find data in a systematic way.

On networks and shared computers, file management is used to control **file permissions**. File permissions control who can see or open a file, write to a file or edit it, and who can delete a file. It is the operating system that asks for confirmation when you try to delete a file.

The question asks you to **explain** and so longer answers are required expanding on the first statement, e.g. it provides an interface and why that interface is needed or will be used.

## Now try this

1  Explain what is meant by multitasking.                                     **(2 marks)**

2  Explain the role of the operating system in multitasking.                   **(2 marks)**

# Operating systems 2

Operating systems control the ways in which users interact with the computer through the user interface and control peripheral devices.

## User interface

The user interface allows the user to communicate with the computer. Many operating systems provide a **Graphical User Interface (GUI)** with **W**indows, **I**cons, drop-down **M**enus and **P**ointers (WIMP). Common GUIs are Windows, iOS and Android. Other interfaces just allow the user to type in commands. These are called **command line interfaces**.

## User management

On networks and shared computers, the operating system **manages users**. Login names and passwords are used to allocate permissions for access to files and folders. User management is often used in organisations to prevent individual users making changes to computer software or making inappropriate use of the computer.

## Peripheral device management

Most computer systems use **peripheral devices** for input and output of data.
Input devices include:

- keyboard
- mouse
- microphone
- webcam
- scanner.

Output devices can include:

- printer
- loudspeaker
- external/internal monitor
- headphones.

External hard drives and network storage devices are also peripherals. All peripherals are controlled by the operating system using programs called **drivers**. The drivers carry out the necessary translations to allow the CPU and the devices to communicate correctly.

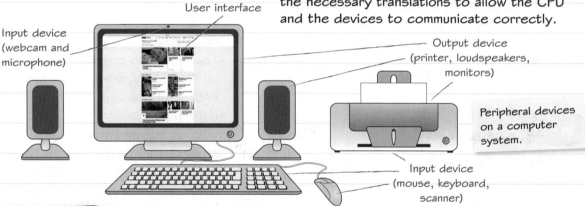

User interface

Input device (webcam and microphone)

Output device (printer, loudspeakers, monitors)

Input device (mouse, keyboard, scanner)

Peripheral devices on a computer system.

## Worked example

One function of the operating system is to manage peripheral devices.

(a) List **two** peripheral devices.    **(2 marks)**

Monitor, printer.

> This question asks you to **list** and to **state** and does not require any explanations or descriptions.

(b) State the name of the software that the operating system uses to communicate with peripheral devices.    **(1 mark)**

Drivers.

> When you get questions about peripheral devices, you could be asked to differentiate them into 'input' and 'output' devices.

## Now try this

 **1** State the role of the user interface.    **(1 mark)**

 **2** Describe the difference between a graphical and a command line interface.    **(2 marks)**

# Utility system software

Utility software is a collection of tools, each of which does a specific job. It helps to **configure the system, analyse** how it is working and **optimise** it to improve its efficiency.

## Encryption software

Encryption is the **scrambling of data** into a form that cannot be understood by unauthorised users. It is used to protect data from unauthorised users of the computer. The encrypted data must be decrypted back to its original form. Encryption/ decryption is carried out using a **cipher** or **key**.

## Data compression software

Data compression software uses algorithms to **reduce the size** of files. This means that less storage space is required. It also makes it easier to transmit files by email or to upload and download them using cloud services. Data compression is commonly used for audio and video files.

**Lossless compression** reduces the size without deleting any of the data. This is important for text files.

**Lossy compression** reduces the size by deleting some of the data.

Find out about the cloud on page 22.

See page 82 for more on compression.

## Defragmentation software

Data is saved to different areas of the disc where there is free space. If the file is larger than the free space in one part of the disc, then part of the file is saved in that space and some more in another area. This is known as **fragmentation**. Over time, this reduces efficiency as more disc accesses are needed to read the complete file. **Defragmentation** software reorganises the files by putting pieces of related data back together, so fewer disc accesses are needed to read the data. This improves performance and can free up more space on the hard disc.

## Backup

Backing up involves copying files to a second medium such as a disc, tape or a cloud service so that they can be **restored** if there are problems with the originals.

They can also compress the data to take up less storage space.

With a **full backup**, all of the specified data is backed up.

With an **incremental backup**, only new files or ones that have changed since the last backup are saved in order to save time.

Some backup software will copy files continuously all the time the computer is switched on. Other software will only run at specified times.

## Worked example

(a) State what is meant by backing up computer data. **(1 mark)**

Backing up involves the copying of data stored on a computer system onto a separate storage device such as a disc or tape.

(b) Describe the difference between a full backup and an incremental backup. **(2 marks)**

In a full backup, all of the data on the storage device is copied.

In an incremental backup, only the data that is new or has been changed is copied.

The questions use the key words **state** and **describe**. Remember: **state** means that you have to give a brief answer without explanation and **describe** means that you have to give a detailed account.

## Now try this

The diagram of a hard disc holding four different files (A, B, C, D) is shown.
Each file is made up of a different number of blocks.

| A2 | C2 | B3 | C1 | D3 | A1 | B1 | D1 | B2 | D2 |
|----|----|----|----|----|----|----|----|----|----|

Redraw the diagram to show the arrangement of the file blocks after defragmentation software has been run.

**(2 marks)**

# Ethical and legal issues

Computer scientists must obey laws and act in ways that are considered moral and good by society.

## Ethics and the law

Everyone, including computer scientists, **must** behave in a legal way and obey any laws that govern the use of computer systems. Some of these laws are covered on pages 36 and 37. Computer scientists **should** behave ethically and act in ways that individuals and societies think of as reflecting good values.

## Difference between ethics and law

| Ethics | Law |
|--------|-----|
| Ethics describe guidelines for computer users to follow. | The law describes **rules** that computer users **must** obey to prevent misuse of computer systems. |
| Ethical principles can be applied anywhere in the world – they are not restricted to national legislation. | Laws may vary from country to country. |
| It is immoral not to follow the ethical code but it is not a crime. | It is **illegal** and constitutes a crime to not follow laws. Computer users must follow the rules or face prosecution. |

## Ethical rules for computer users

Organisations such as the Computer Ethics Institute publish ethical statements for computer professionals and users. Their Ten Commandments of Computer Ethics include:

- Thou shalt not use a computer to harm other people.
- Thou shalt not snoop around in other people's computer files.
- Thou shalt always use a computer in ways that ensure consideration and respect for your fellow humans.

## Codes of conduct for programmers and computer scientists

Professional organisations such as the British Computer Society have developed professional codes of conduct that outline appropriate professional behaviour, and include membership rules such as:

- members should develop their professional skills and competence
- members should never claim a level of competence that they do not possess.

## Worked example

What is legal for computer scientists to do isn't always ethical. Explain the difference between legal and ethical considerations.

**(2 marks)**

Legal requirements are different from country to country and, if they are not obeyed, then a crime has been committed and the person faces prosecution.

Ethical requirements are those that society considers good or moral. Not following them does not lead to prosecution.

The question asks you to **explain** and so a full answer is required with more than one statement about each of the terms.
You may also have questions where you have to put forward your own views about whether a computer scientist has acted in an ethical manner.

## Now try this

A computer scientist has several client companies, both large and small. When she gets requests for assistance and to fix bugs in her software, she has to prioritise how she responds. She could:
- solve each one as it is received
- solve the ones for the large companies first as they pay more money
- decide which are the most serious and solve them first.

Discuss these options with regard to working in an ethical way.

**(4 marks)**

# Cultural issues 1

Computer science technologies have had a profound effect on the ways in which people live, work and relate to each other.

## Stakeholders

A stakeholder is a person or group of people who own or have an interest in a business or organisation.

In a school, the stakeholders include:

- students
- teachers and other employees
- parents
- local community
- local authority.

We are all stakeholders in the society in which we live and, as members, we have both rights from it and duties or responsibilities to it.

The whole population of the world are stakeholders in computer science technologies. This and the following pages show how they are affected in both beneficial and harmful ways.

## Stakeholders and technology

All stakeholders have **responsibilities** to:

- use computer equipment ethically and not use it to harm others
- protect the environment and dispose of old equipment in the correct way.

Stakeholders have **rights** to share in the benefits of using computer equipment. But not all of them do.

## The digital divide

The **digital divide** describes the gap between the digital 'haves' and 'have-nots', where the 'have-nots' have poor or no access to technology. It could be caused by:

- lack of access to broadband
- being unable to afford to access it
- low IT literacy.

## Mobile technology and communication

Mobile technology allows wider communication as it is not restricted to expensive infrastructure (fixed telephone lines).

Mobile communications can include:

- voice, text and media messages
- video conferencing
- emails
- social networking

Social networking sites allow people to communicate wherever they are to:

- instantly publish personal thoughts and ideas
- campaign on social and political issues
- share images, videos and music with friends and family all over the world.

## Worked example

Computer science technologies have changed the ways in which people interact with each other.

Identify **four** computer science technologies that have had an impact on the way in which people socialise. **(4 marks)**

Mobile voice messaging
Text messages
Emails
Video conferencing

The question just asks you to **identify** or **state** and no descriptions or explanations are required.

## Now try this

Explain how computer science technologies can improve the quality of life of elderly people living alone.

**(4 marks)**

# Cultural issues 2

Developments in computer science technologies have had a huge impact on people's access to information and the interconnection of people across the world – globalisation.

## Business, commerce and work

Retailers can **sell** from an online store, which means:

- there is no need to maintain a high street presence
- they can target customers all over the world
- customers can **buy** online from retailers anywhere in the world.

## Entertainment

Computer technologies allow a hugely expanded range of digital television channels, streaming video services and home entertainment systems.

## Working practices

Remote access allows collaborative online working and sharing files. Good broadband allows more home-working, which means:

- less need for office space
- less time wasted travelling to place of work
- more flexible working hours.

## Computer games

Gaming is a huge $100bn a year industry.
Top games can earn more than blockbuster films.

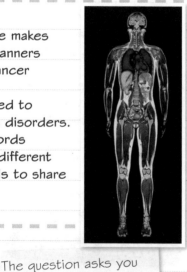

## Education

Computers are used for research, teaching, assessment and management. There are, for example:

- interactive whiteboards.
- virtual learning environments (VLEs).
- ebook versions of textbooks.
- computerised administration.

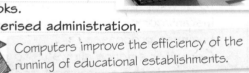

Computers improve the efficiency of the running of educational establishments.

## Medicine

- Modern health care makes use of full body scanners for diagnosis of cancer and heart disease.
- DNA analysis is used to screen for genetic disorders.
- Online patient records make it easier for different health professionals to share information.

## Worked example

List **three** ways in which developments in computer science technologies have had an impact on education. **(3 marks)**

Ebooks give access to additional online content.

Interactive whiteboards enable teachers to use a wider range of multimedia and online resources.

Virtual learning environments enable students to submit homework via the internet and teachers can keep track of student progress.

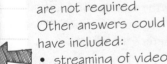

The question asks you to **list** so explanations are not required.
Other answers could have included:
- streaming of videos
- setting work/handing it in online
- administration.

## Now try this

Discuss how the development of broadband and internet technologies has affected people's use of entertainment.

**(8 marks)**

# Environmental issues

The impact of computer science technologies on the environment is both positive and negative.

## Energy consumption

Vast amounts of energy are consumed in:
• production and assembly of computer equipment
• functioning of equipment
• online data storage in data centres
• recycling of equipment.

However, smarter technologies help to protect the environment, e.g. light sensors that turn off lights when they are not needed and route planners that reduce fuel consumption.

Energy is used to run and cool the servers used for online storage. Many are now located in countries such as Norway with cool climates and cheap sustainable energy supplied from hydroelectricity.

Satellite navigation helps drivers choose the quickest routes.

## E-waste

• Waste created by electronic devices may be illegally dumped in landfill sites where toxic waste substances (lead, mercury and cobalt) can get into the land and water.
• Many computer components cannot be recycled or reused.
• Millions of tonnes of e-waste are dumped in developing countries every year.

Illegal tipping of e-waste causes health problems around the world.

## Sustainability

☞ Digital devices contain over 60 different elements. Many are in short supply. It has been estimated that indium will be used up in 10 years, platinum in 15 years and silver in 20 years.

☞ Most of the energy used comes from non-renewable resources – fossil fuels such as coal, gas and oil.

☞ Computers help us develop and produce new sustainable materials and technologies (such as development of new energy sources).

☞ Paperless communication such as email reduces the number of trees cut down.

## Recycling

Sustainability and e-waste issues can be addressed by recycling or reusing old devices:
• elements can be extracted and reused
• some components can be reused
• unwanted items can be donated to poorer countries.

### Efficiencies

✓ Experts from all fields can share research to develop better, smarter solutions. Instant communication speeds up business processes.

✓ Computer science allows us to monitor and study the environment and better understand how it works and how we affect it.

## Worked example

Debbie wants to buy a new PC but is worried about the amount of electricity it will use. State **two** ways in which she could minimise her computer's use of electricity. **(2 marks)**

She should choose an energy efficient device.
She should switch it off when not in use.

Devices kept on standby or sleep mode consume large amounts of energy. It was estimated that wireless routers and laser printers consume about £20 per household worth of electricity per year when sitting idle.

## Now try this

Debbie's computer is running slowly and she wants to replace it with a new one.

 (a) Explain why Debbie should not just throw her old computer in the bin. **(3 marks)**

 (b) Give **two** ways in which Debbie could dispose of her old computer sustainably. **(2 marks)**

# Privacy issues

Computer science technologies have made it possible to monitor the movement and communication of all citizens.

## Monitoring where you are

- **Mobile phone service providers** keep records of calls and texts that are sent and received. The location of a phone can be tracked 24/7 by comparing the phone's signal strength from different phone masts.

- **Passports are scanned** at airports and immigration checkpoints when we travel abroad. Our movements in and out of different countries are monitored.

Epassport gates at an airport.

## Surveillance cameras

- Britain has the largest network of surveillance cameras in Europe. People can be tracked in most cities.
- Automatic Number Plate Recognition (ANPR) makes it possible to track all road vehicles automatically.

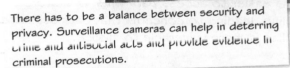

There has to be a balance between security and privacy. Surveillance cameras can help in deterring crime and antisocial acts and provide evidence in criminal prosecutions.

## Monitoring what you do

- Online activity is recorded and used by internet service providers.

All items of browsing history can be monitored and used for targeted advertising. This includes any searches, followed links and items bought online.

- The use of credit cards and debit cards allows the banks to know when, where and how much money you spend.

## Social networking sites

Social networking sites store a vast amount of information about our movements, communications, habits and activities. Care should be taken about what is posted on these sites.

Geotagging from photographs posted online can be used to monitor movements.

---

## Worked example

State **two** ways in which computer science technologies are being used to monitor your location. **(2 marks)**

The location of a GPS-enabled device such as a smart phone can be tracked.

When someone uses an e-passport to enter or leave a country, information about their location is recorded.

The question asks you to **state** so no explanations are needed. Other suitable answers include use of CCTV cameras, credit/debit cards, store loyalty cards, swiping an ID badge to gain admittance to a building.

---

## Now try this

Give **two** arguments in favour of and **two** arguments against the use of surveillance cameras. **(4 marks)**

This question requires you to present the arguments for and against the use of surveillance cameras. How do they help society? How can they be harmful to individuals and personal freedom?

# Legislation 1

Legislation safeguards users' online privacy and security and prevents the misuse of data.

## Data Protection Act 1998

The Data Protection Act 1998 relates to all personal data held by organisations, in paper or electronic form. The Act was put in place to prevent misuse of personal data.

Companies holding our data are required by law:

- to keep it secure
- not to ask for more data than necessary
- not to keep data any longer than necessary
- to keep data accurate and up to date
- not to use the data for any other purpose without our consent.

It is easier to access data when it is stored online, leading to concerns that data submitted online is more vulnerable to misuse.

### Worked example

Adina likes to buy clothes online. The websites she uses hold her personal data.
Describe the law that protects her data.  **(2 marks)**

The Data Protection Act 1998 protects Adina's personal data by ensuring that it is kept secure, accurate, up to date and private.

Make sure that you learn details of the actual legislation so that you can list them in the answers. You should give more than just general details about security.

## Data subject rights

Many organisations store personal details electronically (such as the government, the NHS, social networking sites, schools and online retailers). Everyone whose data is stored is a **data subject** and has the right to:

**1** inspect and check the data held, but the organisations can charge for this

**2** demand that incorrect information is amended

**3** demand that the data is not used in any way that could harm or distress

**4** demand that any data held by the organisation is not used for direct marketing.

## The Computer Misuse Act 1990

With the widespread use of the internet, it is now easier to remotely log into a network and use someone's computer and steal or corrupt data.

The Computer Misuse Act lists three levels of crime:

**1** **Unauthorised access to computer material**. This includes logging into another person's computer with their password without their permission and stealing documents and programs.

**2** **Unauthorised modification of computer material**. This includes destroying or corrupting a user's files, modifying system files or creating a virus or other malware.

**3** **Unauthorised access to a computer with intent**. This includes gaining access to financial or administrative records and using the information to commit a further crime.

### Now try this

Many organisations store customers' personal details.
Explain the rights of the customers with regard to this data.  **(3 marks)**

# Legislation 2

Digital systems make it easy to share content, but laws are needed to ensure that original work is not stolen or misused.

## Copyright, Designs and Patents Act 1988

The Act protects people's original work from being used without their permission. All original work is copyright, including everything that is freely available to download from the internet. The person who **creates a work owns the copyright** and is the only person who has the right to reproduce, adapt or sell it.

Creators of inventions can apply for **patents** that **prevent others from making, using or selling the invention** without their permission.

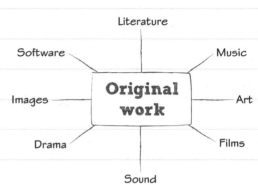

## Freedom of Information Act 2000

The Act creates a right of access to information held by public authorities, which includes:

- central and local government
- the health service
- schools, colleges and universities
- the police and courts.

Anyone can make a request for information. If the holder refuses, an appeal can be made to the **Information Commissioner**.

## Creative Commons licensing

Creative Commons licences give the public permission to share and use work under certain conditions:

- **Public domain**: there are no restrictions. Work can be used without permission or attribution for any purpose.
- **Attribution commercial licence**: work can be used, distributed and copied as long as the creator is given credit for having created it.
- **Attribution-non-commercial licence**: work can be used, distributed and copied for non-commercial purposes with suitable attribution.

The licences give people the right to share, use, and build upon a work that an artist, musician or writer has created.

---

### Worked example

State **two** legal sanctions that could be applied to users for the illegal copying and sharing of files. **(2 marks)**

The user could be prosecuted, fined or sent to prison.

The user could be prevented from using the internet by their internet service provider.

Remember the difference between ethical and legal considerations. If the question had asked for the ethical effects of illegal copying you could have mentioned:

- Creators of the music lose the money they need to create and record their music.
- It can lead to unemployment because of loss of revenue.

---

### Now try this

Ann wants to allow other people to use the graphic images she has produced.
Explain why a Creative Commons licence is suitable for this purpose. **(2 marks)**

# Proprietry and open-source software

Computer users have a choice of commercially-available software, which has to be paid for, or open-source software, which is free to use.

## Proprietary software

Proprietary software is **commercially** produced by an organisation for a profit, e.g. Windows, OS X, Microsoft Office.

👍 It is developed professionally and carefully tested.

👍 Support is provided to keep customers happy so that they will keep using the software.

👍 Books, magazine articles and online tutorials give advice and instruction.

👍 Updates and bug fixes meet the needs and suggestions of the users.

👎 User licences apply conditions on the ways the software can be used and distributed.

👎 The source code cannot be modified by users.

👎 The person or organisation who created it maintains exclusive control over it.

👎 It is developed for the majority of users and may not meet individual needs.

👎 It has to be paid for, it is not free.

👎 Support and updates may be expensive.

## Open-source software

Open source is software whose source code is available for modification or enhancement by anyone, e.g. Open Office, Linux, Android, Ubuntu.

👍 Users can study the source code to see how the software works.

👍 Users can change and upgrade the software.

👍 Under the licence, users can pass on the software to other users for no charge.

👍 It is free to use.

👍 Users can modify the source code to adapt it to their needs.

👍 Constant upgrades are available.

👍 There is a community of dedicated enthusiasts who will provide help and support.

👎 May not appear as professional as proprietary software or have such a user-friendly interface.

👎 Specialist knowledge may be needed.

---

## Worked example

A school has decided to install an open-source software suite on its computers rather than a proprietary version.

Describe **two** advantages for the school in doing this. **(4 marks)**

It is usually free to use and this will save the school a lot of money.
The licence allows users to see and modify the source code and the school will be able to customise it to their needs or use the code for teaching purposes.

The advantages must be **described**. You cannot just say 'It is free to use' but the advantage of that must be given.
Other answers could have included:
- There is a large user base of dedicated enthusiasts who will supply free help and advice through online forums.
- Users are allowed to modify the code and pass it on to other users free of charge and there will be a constant supply of free upgrades.

---

## Now try this

Charles uses word processing and spreadsheet software to help run his business. He is a novice and has no experience of using computers or software.

Give **two** reasons why proprietary software would be better for this user than open-source software.

**(2 marks)**

# Computational thinking

Computational thinking is a term used to describe the thought processes involved in understanding problems and formulating solutions in such a way that they can be carried out by computers.

## Decomposition

Decomposition reduces a problem into sub-problems or components. These smaller parts are easier to understand and solve. This is an example of a divide-and-conquer approach.

| **Problem** |
| Create a 'snakes and ladders' computer game |

⬇

| **Sub-problems** |

→ | Design of playing area |

→ | Positions of snakes and ladders |

→ | Dice throw for each player |

→ | Movement of each player on board |

→ | Movement up ladders and down snakes |

→ | How does a player finish? |

## Algorithmic thinking

Algorithmic thinking is a subset of computational thinking that involves defining a clear set of instructions to solve a problem. Once a successful solution to a problem has been found, it can be used repeatedly for the same problem. For example, the process of calculating the mean of a set of numbers is always the same irrespective of how many numbers and what they are – add up all the numbers and divide the total by the number in the set.

## Abstraction

Abstraction identifies essential elements that must be included in the computer models of real-life situations and discards inessential ones.

For a computer model of 'Snakes and Ladders', the sub-problem 'Dice throw for each player' includes the essential element: 'Generate a random number between 1 and 6'.

Inessential elements would include whether you use a shaker, how long you shake it for and how far you throw the dice.

| Real life | Computer model |
|-----------|----------------|
| Dice throw for each player | Generate a random number between 1 and 6. |
| Move counter | Calculate new position. |
| Move up a ladder or down a snake | Calculate if user is in same position as start of a ladder or snake. Calculate new position. |

## Pattern recognition

Pattern recognition is sometimes called **generalisation**, which is used to:

- identify where constructs such as **selection** and **iteration** can be used
- identify where sections of code can be reused (**functions** and **procedures**)
- recognise a problem that is similar to one you have solved in the past
- reuse code, functions and procedures from past programs to carry out similar functions in a new program.

## Worked example

In a computer 'Snakes and Ladders' game, there is a function named 'dice throw' which is called whenever it is a user's turn.

Give a reason why this function is an abstraction. **(1 mark)**

The 'dice throw' function is an abstraction because if focuses on the essential purpose of throwing a dice, i.e. to generate a number between 1 and 6, and ignores non-essential aspects of the problem, e.g. the colour of the dice or whether or not a shaker is used.

## Now try this

Describe what is meant by the following terms:
- decomposition
- algorithmic thinking. **(4 marks)**

# Algorithms

Algorithms provide precise instructions needed to solve a problem. All computer programs are algorithms. An algorithm is a step-by-step procedure for solving a problem or carrying out a task.

## Uses for algorithms

Algorithms are often used to improve efficiency by removing the need for human input. For example automatic-pilot systems in aircraft and share trading on the stock market. A computer following an algorithm can decide which deal to make far more quickly than a human and a split second difference can be worth millions of pounds.

## Constructs of an algorithm

There are three constructs used in an algorithm – **sequence**, **selection** and **iteration**. Here is an algorithm for a guessing game.

1 Person A thinks of a number between 1 and 20.

2 Person B makes a guess.

3 If the guess is too great:
   (a) person A says 'Too high'
   (b) go to step 2.

4 If the guess is too small:
   (a) person A says 'Too low'
   (b) go to step 2.

5 If the guess is correct:
   (a) person A says 'Correct'.

**Sequence** – instructions need to be given in the correct order for the game to be played successfully.

**Selection** – decisions have to be made and a course of action selected.

**Iteration** – previous steps are repeated until there is a desired outcome (in this case, until there is a correct guess).

### Worked example

Write an algorithm to make a cup of instant coffee. It should be annotated to show where sequence, selection and iteration have been used.    **(5 marks)**

1 Fill kettle with water. (sequence)

2 Turn on kettle. (sequence)

3 Place coffee in the cup. (sequence)

4 Check if the water is boiling. (selection)

5 If water is not boiling go back to step 4. (iteration)

6 Pour water into the cup. (sequence)

7 If needed, add milk and sugar. (selection)

8 Stir. (sequence)

## Reusing algorithms

Once an algorithm has been written, it can be reused with slight changes for solving similar problems – which is much quicker than starting from scratch each time.

Selection occurs when a decision has to be made and iteration is used when a sequence of activities has to be repeated.

### Now try this

Algorithms use selection and iteration.

Define what is meant by:
• selection
• iteration.    **(2 marks)**

# Algorithms – pseudocode

Algorithms can be displayed using pseudocode.

## Pseudocode

- Pseudocode is a way of expressing an algorithm in structured English that resembles a computer language.
- There are many different varieties of pseudocode but, in your exam, questions will be written using the OCR version.
- You may provide answers in any style of pseudocode as long as the meaning could be reasonably understood by a competent programmer.

## Use of pseudocode

- ✓ Pseudocode uses commands, keywords and structures similar to those found in computer languages.
- ✓ Pseudocode cannot be understood by computers, but is used to develop the **logic** of the algorithm without having to bother about **syntax** (the rules of grammar such as spelling or punctuation).
- ✓ A human can follow the logic of an algorithm even if there are spelling mistakes or missing brackets but a computer cannot execute code if there are similar syntax errors.
- ✓ A solution in pseudocode is converted into a programming language such as Python or Java.

## Example of pseudocode

This pseudocode shows an algorithm for calculating the cost of sending parcels. The pseudocode shows the logic of the algorithm.

Variables have been used e.g. parcel, weight and excess.

```
parcel = "y"
while parcel == "y" // The loop will run while parcel = "y"
  weight = input("Please enter the weight of the parcel.")
  if weight <= 2 then
    cost = 2 //Parcels up to 2kg cost £2
  else
    excess = weight - 2
    cost = 2 + excess*3 //Over 2kg, the cost is £2 plus £3
                         per additional kg
  endif
  print(cost)
  parcel = input("Press 'y' to process another parcel.")
endwhile
```

Indefinite iteration using a while loop as the number of parcels to be processed is not known at the start.

Comments are included in pseudocode using the // symbol. Comments are used by programmers to help others to follow their logic, and to act as a reminder of the logic. It is good practice to include comments.

Indenting helps with the logic of the algorithm by showing dependency – everything inside the else block (lines 7 and 8) is indented to show the lines dependent on this instruction. The pseudocode is not going to be executed by a computer, so indentation is not strictly necessary but it makes the code easier to understand.

The user is asked if they want the loop to run again. It will stop if the input is other than y.

---

## Now try this

Display as pseudocode an algorithm that will find the sum of 10 numbers entered by a user and output the result. Use suitable comments and indentation.

**(6 marks)**

# Algorithms – flow diagrams

Algorithms can be displayed as flow diagrams (also known as flowcharts).

## Symbols used in flow diagrams

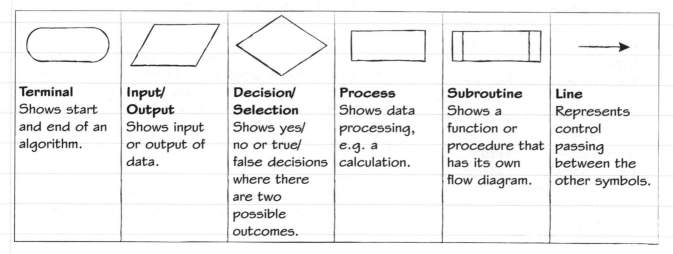

| Terminal | Input/ Output | Decision/ Selection | Process | Subroutine | Line |
|---|---|---|---|---|---|
| Shows start and end of an algorithm. | Shows input or output of data. | Shows yes/ no or true/ false decisions where there are two possible outcomes. | Shows data processing, e.g. a calculation. | Shows a function or procedure that has its own flow diagram. | Represents control passing between the other symbols. |

## Flow diagrams in use

The costs of sending a parcel by courier varies according to the weight of the parcel:

if a parcel weighs <= 2kg, the cost is £2

if a parcel weighs > 2kg, it costs £2 + £3 × excess weight.

This flow diagram represents an algorithm for calculating the cost of sending parcels.

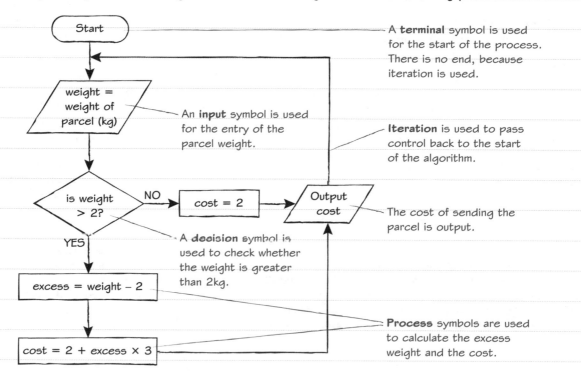

A **terminal** symbol is used for the start of the process. There is no end, because iteration is used.

An **input** symbol is used for the entry of the parcel weight.

**Iteration** is used to pass control back to the start of the algorithm.

The cost of sending the parcel is output.

A **decision** symbol is used to check whether the weight is greater than 2kg.

**Process** symbols are used to calculate the excess weight and the cost.

---

### Now try this

Draw a flow chart for an algorithm to find the sum of 10 numbers and output the result.      **(5 marks)**

# Standard searching algorithms – linear search

When large amounts of data are searched, it is essential that the searching algorithm is as efficient as possible. Standard search algorithms include **linear** and **binary** searches.

See page 44 for more information on binary searches.

## Linear search

A linear search is **sequential**. This algorithm starts at the beginning of the list and moves through item by item until it finds the matching item or reaches the end of the list. To find the number 37 in a list, a linear search would start at the first entry (20) and simply move to the next item until it finds 37 (or reaches the end of the list).

indices

| 0 | 1 | 2 | 3 | 4 | 5 | 6 | 7 | 8 |
|---|---|---|---|---|---|---|---|---|
| 20 | 35 | 37 | 40 | 45 | 50 | 51 | 55 | 67 |
| ↑ | ↑ | ↑ | | | | | | |
| ≠ | ≠ | = | | | | | | |

The number is found on the third comparison at index 2.
Remember: indices start at 0.

### Brute force

A linear search is an example of a brute-force algorithm. It does not use any specialist techniques, only raw computing power. It is not an efficient method as each search starts at the beginning and keeps going until the item is found or the end of the list is reached.

## The efficiency of a linear search

If there is a list of 500 items:

- In the **best case**, the search item is the first item found.

- In the **worst case**, the search item is the last item found – number 500.

Average case: $\dfrac{(500 + 1)}{2} = 250.5$

The smaller the list the more efficient the linear search.

## Worked example

Describe in words an algorithm for carrying out a linear search. **(6 marks)**

1 If the length of the list is zero, stop.
2 Start at the beginning of the list.
3 Compare the list item with the search criterion.
4 If they are the same, then stop.
5 If they are not the same, then move to the next item.
6 Repeat steps 3 to 5 until the end of the list is reached.

It is best to number the steps in case iteration is needed. In this answer, the step numbers are used for the iteration command in step 6.

Remember that the length of the list must be checked to ensure that there are some items to search (step 1). When coding this algorithm a Boolean flag would be set to 'yes' when the item was found so that no further searching would take place.

## Now try this

Find out more about arrays on page 59.

Design an algorithm expressed in pseudocode to ask a user for a search item and carry out a linear search on data stored in an array to find that item. **(6 marks)**

# Standard searching algorithms – binary search

A binary search compares the search item with the median item in a list, repeatedly splitting the list in half until the item is found or there are no more items left to search.

## Binary search

To use a binary search, the list must have already been sorted into ascending order. A binary search uses a divide-and-conquer strategy to increase its efficiency:

- select the median
- compare it with the search item
- if the search item is **lower**, discard the median and the **higher items**
- if the search item is **higher**, discard the median and **lower items**
- recalculate the new median
- repeat this process until the search item is found (or is not found) in the list.

## Median values

- ✓ The **median** is the middle item in a list. In a list of 13 items, the median item is the 7th item in the sorted list.
- ✓ If there are an even number of items, then the one to the left of the median can be used, e.g. if there are 10 numbers then the 6th can be used.
- ✓ Lists of numbers need to be sorted in numerical order.
- ✓ Lists of words or text strings need to be sorted into alphabetical order.

---

## Worked example

Numbers have been written onto 11 cards that have then been placed face down in ascending order. Show the stages in a binary search to see if the number 28 is on one of the cards. **(4 marks)**

| ☐ | ☐ | ☐ | ☐ | ☐ | 36 | ☐ | ☐ | ☐ | ☐ | ☐ |

◀ The median card is selected and turned over. The number on the median card is **higher** than the search item, so the sub-list to the **left** is used.

| ☐ | ☐ | 17 | ☐ | ☐ |

◀ The new median is selected. The number on the median card is **lower** than the search item, so the sub-list to the **right** is used.

| 29 | ☐ |

◀ The left card is turned over. The new median is higher than the search item but there is no sub-list to the left. This confirms that the search item is not in the list.

The search has confirmed that the number 28 is not on any of the cards.

---

## Now try this

Describe the stages in applying a binary search to the following list to find the number 17.

3, 5, 9, 14, 17, 21, 27, 31, 35, 37, 39, 40, 42

**(4 marks)**

# Comparing linear and binary searches

The binary search algorithm is more efficient than a linear search but the list has to be sorted into ascending or descending order.

## The efficiency of linear vs binary search

The table shows a comparison for a list of 500 items.

| | Linear search | Number of selections | Binary search | Number of selections |
|---|---|---|---|---|
| Best case | The search item is the first one. | 1 | The search item is the median. | 1 |
| Worst case | The search item is the last one: number 500 | 500 | Assuming that the median was too large each time, the following would be selected: 250, 125, 63, 32, 16, 8, 4, 2, 1 | 10 |
| Average case | $\dfrac{(500 + 1)}{2} = 250.5$  That would mean 251 searches. | 251 | $\dfrac{(9 + 1)}{2} = 5.0$  That would mean 6 searches. | 6 |

---

**Worked example**

Describe **one** benefit and **one** drawback of using a binary search rather than a linear search.

**(4 marks)**

A benefit of the binary search is that it uses a strategy to minimise the number of comparisons that are made and is therefore more efficient than a linear search when there are a lot of items in the list.

A drawback of using the binary search is that the data must first be sorted into ascending order. Sorting the data will take time and reduce the overall efficiency.

A binary search uses a strategy to reduce the number of comparisons needed but a linear search starts at the first item and checks every one until the item is found or it gets to the end of the list.

---

**Now try this**

A student has the following names of friends stored in a list.

| Alice | Ann | Claire | David | Mary | Matt | Peter | Stephen | Zoe |
|---|---|---|---|---|---|---|---|---|

Show the stages of a binary search to find the name Ann in the above data.    **(2 marks)**

# Standard sorting algorithms – bubble sort

Data must be sorted into order to make it easier to understand and to use. There are many different sorting algorithms. The bubble sort algorithm compares adjacent data items and orders them. Several passes may be needed to sort the whole list.

## Order of sorting

Data can be sorted into:

- **ascending** order: 1, 2, 3, 4, 5 or a, b, c, d
- **descending** order: 5, 4, 3, 2, 1 or d, c, b, a

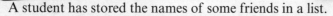

## How bubble sort works

A bubble sort algorithm starts at the beginning of the list and examines the first two items.

**FIRST PASS**

(2) (1) 3 6 5 4 ——— They are **not** in the correct order so they are **swapped**.

1 (2) (3) 6 5 4 ——— The second and third items are compared. They are in the correct order so they are left in place.

1 2 (3) (6) 5 4 ——— The next two items (3 and 6) are compared. These are in the correct order and left in place.

1 2 3 (6) (5) 4 ——— The next two items (6 and 5) are compared. They are not in the correct order so they are **swapped**.

1 2 3 5 (6) (4) ——— The next two items (6 and 4) are compared. They are not in the correct order so they are **swapped**.

1 2 3 5 4 6 ——— When the algorithm reaches the end of the list, the first pass has been completed.

**SECOND PASS**

1 2 3 (5) (4) 6 ——— The first, second and third items are in the correct order so they are left in place. The next items (5 and 4) are compared and swapped.

1 2 3 4 5 6 ——— When the alogrithm reaches the end of the list the second pass has been completed. The algorithm will continue with more passes until no swaps are made. The list will then have been sorted into order.

---

### Worked example

A student has stored the names of some friends in a list.

| David | Claire | Stefan | Sophie | Matt |

Show the stages of a bubble sort when applied to this data to sort it into ascending order. **(5 marks)**

Pass 1
Claire, David, Stefan, Sophie, Matt
Claire, David, Stefan, Sophie, Matt
Claire, David, Sophie, Stefan, Matt
Claire, David, Sophie, Matt, Stefan
Pass 2
Claire, David, Matt, Sophie, Stefan
Pass 3
Claire, David, Matt, Sophie, Stefan

All the comparisons in Pass 1 are given even if there was no swap (such as David/Stefan). Names swapped are underlined. The names of the passes have also been given.

---

### Now try this

Show the stages of a bubble sort when applied to the following data to sort it into ascending order:
4 1 2 6 3 5

**(5 marks)**

# Standard sorting algorithms – insertion sort

The insertion sort algorithm examines each data item in turn and moves it to its correct position.

## How insertion sort works

The algorithm starts by examining the **second** item in the list.
If this sort item is **lower** than the first item, the sort item moves in front of the first item.

| 6 | 3 | 1 | 2 | 5 | 4 |
|---|---|---|---|---|---|

The third item is lower than the first two and is moved into its correct position. The others are moved along to the right.

| 3 | 6 | 1 | 2 | 5 | 4 |
|---|---|---|---|---|---|

The **fourth** item is lower than the two items immediately to its left (3 and 6), but greater than the next term left (1), and is moved into its correct position. The others are moved along to the right.

| 1 | 3 | 6 | 2 | 5 | 4 |
|---|---|---|---|---|---|

The **fifth** item is examined and is moved into position.

| 1 | 2 | 3 | 6 | 5 | 4 |
|---|---|---|---|---|---|

The **sixth** and last item in the list is moved into position.

| 1 | 2 | 3 | 5 | 6 | 4 |
|---|---|---|---|---|---|

| 1 | 2 | 3 | 4 | 5 | 6 |
|---|---|---|---|---|---|

The items are now in ascending order.

## Worked example

A student has stored their scores in a list: 7 5 3 6 8 10 9 4

Show the stages of an insertion sort when applied to this data.  **(5 marks)**

```
5 7 3 6 8 10 9 4
3 5 7 6 8 10 9 4
3 5 6 7 8 10 9 4
3 5 6 7 8 10 9 4
3 5 6 7 8 10 9 4
3 5 6 7 8 9 10 4
3 4 5 6 7 8 9 10
```

All the comparisons have been shown and the items moved are shown underlined.

## Now try this

Show the stages of an insertion sort when used to sort the following list of names into ascending order.
Mai  Devi  Sanjita  Alice  Maalik  Catherine  Jane        **(5 marks)**

# Standard sorting algorithms – merge sort

The merge sort algorithm breaks a list into its component parts and then builds it up again with them in the correct order.

## How merge sort works

**1** The algorithm breaks the list into two, and then these into two, over and over again.

| 6 | 3 | 5 | 1 | 8 | 2 | 4 | 7 |

| 6 | 3 | 5 | 1 |    | 8 | 2 | 4 | 7 |

| 6 | 3 |    | 5 | 1 |    | 8 | 2 |    | 4 | 7 |

| 6 | | 3 | | 5 | | 1 | | 8 | | 2 | | 4 | | 7 |

**2** The items are then reassembled in the same way but in ascending order.
3 is compared with 6, 5 is compared with 1, 2 is compared with 8, 4 is compared with 7 and they are placed in the correct order.

| 3 | 6 |     | 1 | 5 |     | 2 | 8 |     | 4 | 7 |

**3** The leftmost items in each list are the lower items of those lists and the algorithm compares them – in this case, 3 with 1. The 1 is inserted in the new list and the 3 is then compared with the second number of the right-hand list (5). The 3 is inserted and the 5 is compared with the second number of the left-hand list (6). The same method is used for 2, 8, 4, 7 to form two lists.

| 1 | 3 | 5 | 6 |        | 2 | 4 | 7 | 8 |

**4** The two lists are combined to make a final list in the correct order.

| 1 | 2 | 3 | 4 | 5 | 6 | 7 | 8 |

---

**Worked example**

Describe how data is sorted into ascending order using the merge sort algorithm.     **(2 marks)**

The list is divided into two repeatedly until each list has only one item. The lists are then progressively merged with the items in ascending order.

### Recursion

Repeating a process using the results of the first application is called **recursion**.
The list is divided into two and then each part is divided into two, and so on. The results are then **recursively** reassembled in ascending order. Recursion is often used in algorithms and can be implemented by creating a function that calls itself instead of returning to the main program.

See pages 63 and 64 for more information on functions.

---

**Now try this**

Show the stages of a merge sort when used to sort the following list of numbers into ascending order.
38   27   43   3   9   82   10
     **(5 marks)**

# Interpreting, correcting and completing algorithms

It is often difficult to look at an algorithm produced by another programmer and understand what it does and how it does it.

## Dry runs

A dry run is a method used to investigate the **functioning** of an algorithm. It is a mental or pencil and paper run-through of an algorithm that does one step at a time. The following are examined for each step:

- the inputs needed
- the data processing
- the outputs.

A dry run can help you to understand an algorithim and also to find any errors.

## Trace tables

While the dry run is being worked through, it is helpful to use a trace table in which to write down the values of each variable, input and output and how they change as the program is running. A trace table has columns for each of the variables and rows for each of the steps in the algorithm.

## An algorithm and trace table

A student has written an algorithm to carry out a linear search that outputs "Found" if a particular search item is found in a given list. She tests the algorithm with the following data:

3, 6, 9, 13, 17, 21

She uses the number 13 as the search item.

The trace table below shows the values of the different variables compared with the search item.

```
list = [3, 6, 9, 13, 17, 21]
found = false
item = input("Enter search value.")
for index = 0 to list.length - 1
  if item == list[index] then
    found = true
    print("Found")
  endif
next index
```

The variable found contains the value false at the start of the algorithm and is changed to true if the search item is found.

The variable item has the value 13 throughout the running of the algorithm.

Columns are used for the variables and the output.

| item | found | index | list[index] | output |
|------|-------|-------|-------------|--------|
| 13 | false | 0 | 3 | |
| | false | 1 | 6 | |
| | false | 2 | 9 | |
| | true | 3 | 13 | Found |
| | true | 4 | 17 | |
| | true | 5 | 21 | |

The output when the search item is found.

The variable Index increments from 0 to 5, as the length of the array is equal to 6.

The data items at each index position.

## Now try this

Create a trace table for the following algorithm.

```
number = 3
for index = 1 to 3
  number = number + index
  print(number)
next index
```

**(4 marks)**

# Using trace tables

Trace tables have columns for each of the variables and input and output values.

Investigate the following algorithm and complete a trace table using these values.
At the start of the following algorithm, X = 2 and Y = 3

```
Z = X + Y
while X < Z
   X = X + 1
   Y = Y + X
endwhile
print(Y)
```

**(4 marks)**

| Z | X | Y | output |
|---|---|---|--------|
| 5 | 3 | 6 | |

 A table with columns for X, Y, Z and the output is needed. The variables are shown in the order in which they appear in the algorithm.

| Z | X | Y | output |
|---|---|---|--------|
| 5 | 3 | 6 | |

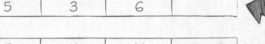 In the first iteration, Z = 5 (2 + 3) and, as X is less than Z (2 < 5), both X and Y will be incremented as instructed in the algorithm.

| Z | X | Y | output |
|---|---|---|--------|
| 5 | 3 | 6 | |
| 5 | 4 | 10 | |

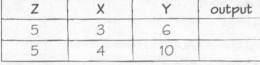 In the next iteration, Z is still equal to 5 as it is not incremented in the loop. X is still less than Z (3 < 5), so X and Y are both incremented as before.

| Z | X | Y | output |
|---|---|---|--------|
| 5 | 3 | 6 | |
| 5 | 4 | 10 | |
| 5 | 5 | 15 | |

 X is still less than Z so there will be another iteration.

The 'while' loop will run while X is less than Z. Z is calculated before the loop starts and so will never change and is equal to the sum of the starting values of X and Y. On the last turn of the loop (when X = 4), it will be incremented to 5 and will then stop.

| Z | X | Y | output |
|---|---|---|--------|
| 5 | 3 | 6 | |
| 5 | 4 | 10 | |
| 5 | 5 | 15 | |
| | | | 15 |

X is now equal to Z so the program execution will break out of the loop.
The value of Y will be printed.

Create a trace table for the following algorithm.

```
number = 3
print (number)
for index = 1 to 3
   number = number + 6
   print(number)
next x
```

**(4 marks)**

# Variables and constants

Variables and constants are used to store values in algorithms and programs.

Variables and constants have names or **identifiers**.

Identifiers describe the data being stored.

- **Short** identifiers are easier to spell correctly each time they are used.
- **Long** identifiers can be used if they are more descriptive e.g. firstName.

Identifiers cannot be the same as reserved words such as print or while.

Variables **can change** while a program is running.
Constants **must not change** while a program is running.

Values are assigned in **assignment statements** using the = symbol.
firstName = "David" or
pricePerKilo = 30.

The variable value can be changed as the program is running e.g.
pricePerKilo = pricePerKilo * 2
would increase the value to 60.

> **A variable, e.g.
> PricePerKilo = 30
> or a constant, e.g.
> const Pi = 3.142**

Variable and constant identifiers must be consistent throughout the program.

**Camel case** uses lower and upper case characters. (FirstName or PricePerKilo)

The first word can be lower case.
(firstName or pricePerKilo)

In **snake case** the words are linked with an underscore. (first_name or price_per_kilo)

Constants are assigned as const Pi - 3.142 or const inchToCm = 2.54, for example and used in calculations:
areaOfCircle = Pi * radius ^ 2.

---

## Assignments

An assignment is the association of a piece of data with a variable or constant, e.g. index = 0. Often the assignment is done as an **input**, e.g.

```
name = input("Please enter your
name.")
```

The value assigned to a variable can be **output** to the user, e.g. print(name). This will output the value stored in the variable name rather than outputting the word "name".

**Worked example**

Identify the variables that are used in this algorithm and state the purpose of each.

```
length = input ("Enter the length of
the rectangle.")
width = input ("Enter the width of
the rectangle.")
area = length * width
print(area)
```
**(6 marks)**

The variables are:

length, width and area.

length and width store values that are input by the user, and area stores the result of multiplying the length by the width.

---

**Now try this**

A student is writing an algorithm that allows a user to input their marks for five tests and then calculates the average mark.

List suitable variables that could be used in the algorithm.      **(1 mark)**

# Arithmetic operators

Operators are used in algorithms to specify how values are to be manipulated.

## Arithmetic operators in algorithms and programs

Arithmetic operators are used to perform calculations in algorithms and programs. The arithmetic operators in the OCR pseudocode are shown below.

| Operator | Function | Example |
|---|---|---|
| + | addition | 13 + 9 = 22 <br> totalScore = score1 + score2 + score3 |
| - | subtraction | 24 - 11 = 13 <br> moneyLeft = totalMoney - moneySpent |
| * | multiplication | 6 * 9 = 54 <br> moneyTaken = numberSold * unitPrice |
| / | division | 36 / 5 = 5.2 <br> numberSold = moneyTaken / unitPrice |
| MOD | **Modulus** division <br> Returns the **remainder** after the division of one number by another | 17 MOD 3 divides 17 by 3 and returns 2 as <br> 17/3 = 5 with a remainder of 2. <br> remainder = number MOD 2 |
| DIV | **Quotient** division <br> Returns the quotient or the lowest integer | 11 DIV 4 = 2 <br> completeHours = minutes DIV 60 |
| ^ | Exponential <br> powers of | 3 ^ 3 = 27 <br> area = Pi * radius ^ 2 |

## Order of operations

You need to use the correct order of operations in a calculation (BIDMAS).
**B**rackets
**I**ndices or powers
**D**ivision
**M**ultiplication
**A**ddition
**S**ubtraction

## Using BIDMAS

The equation

```
number = 3^2 * 12 / (3*2) + 6
```

would be evaluated in this order:

| | |
|---|---|
| 3^2 * 12 / 6 + 6 | brackets (3 × 2) = 6 |
| 9 * 12 / 6 + 6 | index $3^2$ = 9 |
| 9 * 2 + 6 | division 12 ÷ 6 = 2 |
| 18 + 6 | multiplication 9 × 2 = 18 |
| 24 | addition 18 + 6 = 24 |

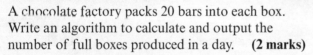

**Worked example**

A chocolate factory packs 20 bars into each box. Write an algorithm to calculate and output the number of full boxes produced in a day. **(2 marks)**

```
numberOfBars = input ("Enter number of
bars produced.")
numberOfBoxes = numberOfBars DIV 20
  print(numberOfBoxes + "full boxes
have been produced.")
```

In the exam, you will be expected to apply your knowledge and use arithmetic operators in algorithms rather than being asked to evaluate equations.

In this example, the DIV operator has been used as the algorithm has to output the number of full boxes.

**Now try this**

Write an algorithm in pseudocode that would allow a user to:
- input the number of items sold by a shop each day for 3 days
- calculate the total number of items sold
- calculate the mean number of items sold each day as an integer. **(3 marks)**

# Comparison operators

Comparison operators (or relational operators) are used to compare different items of data.

## Examples of comparison operators

| Comparison operator | Function | Example |
|---|---|---|
| == | **Equal to**<br>Checks if two values are equal. Two equal signs are used to distinguish it from assigning a value to a variable. | `if length == width then`<br>`   print("It is a square.")`<br>`endif` |
| != | **Not equal to**<br>Checks if two values are not equal to each other. | `if length != width then`<br>`   print("It is not a square.")`<br>`endif` |
| < | **Less than**<br>Checks if one value is less than another. | `if myHeight < yourHeight then`<br>`   print("You are taller than me.")`<br>`endif` |
| <= | **Less than or equal to**<br>Checks if one value is less than or equal to another. | `if number <= 10 then`<br>`   print("The number is less than 11.")`<br>`endif` |
| > | **Greater than**<br>Checks if one value is greater than another. | `if myHeight > yourHeight then`<br>`   print("I am taller than you.")`<br>`endif` |
| >= | **Greater than or equal to**<br>Checks if one value is greater than or equal to another. | `if score >= passMark then`<br>`   print("You have passed.")`<br>`endif` |

## Worked example

Write an algorithm in pseudocode which asks the user to enter a number between 1 and 10 and then states if it is higher, lower or equal to 5. **(4 marks)**

```
number = input("Enter a number between
1 and 10")
if number > 5 then
   print("Higher than 5.")
elseif number < 5 then
   print("Lower than 5.")
else
   print("You entered 5.")
endif
```

## Comparing strings

These operators can be used with strings as well as numbers. The strings are compared alphabetically.

For example,

D is higher in the alphabet than C so David is greater than Catherine.

"Db" is greater than "Da".

Relational operators are used in selection using if...elseif...else statements to compare the values of variables. The > and < operators have been used but the == operator is not needed as the number must equal 5 if it is not less than nor greater than 5.

## Now try this

Write an algorithm, in pseudocode, that allows a user to enter two values as `value1` and `value2` and which will switch the values, if necessary, so that they are in ascending order.

**(2 marks)**

# Boolean operators

Boolean operators are used to combine statements, or operands, which can be evaluated as true or false.

## The AND operator

Using the AND operator ensures that the overall statement is true only if **all** of the individual statements are true.

```
If number1 == 3 AND number2 == 6 AND
number3 == 10 then
   result = true
endif
```

For a result to be true they **all** have to be true – they have to be equal to 3, 6 and 10.

## The OR operator

Using the OR operator ensures that the overall statement is true if **any** of the individual statements are true.

```
if number1 == 3 OR number2 == 6 OR
number3 == 10 then
   result = true
endif
```

For a result to be true then any one or all of the statements has to be true, e.g. if number1 = 3 then the overall statement is true even if the other numbers are not 6 and 10.

## The NOT operator

The NOT operator is used to reverse the logical state of the other operators.

```
if NOT (number1 == 3 OR number2 == 6)
then
   result == true
endif
```

Without the NOT operator, the statement would be true if either number1 = 3 **or** number2 = 6. Therefore, with the NOT operator, **both** must be false for the overall statement to be true. Note the use of brackets.

> The OR statement in the algorithm is enclosed in brackets to make it easier for users to follow the logic and to determine the order in which the expressions are evaluated.

State the output from this algorithm with these values. At the start of the algorithm X = 2, Y = 6 and Z = 9

```
if (X == 3 OR Y == 6) AND NOT (Z == 9)
   print("Conditions are met.")
else
   print("Conditions not met.")
endif                            (1 mark)
```

The output will be "Conditions not met"

> The OR statement in brackets is true as Y is equal to 6.
> But the overall statement is false as Z is equal to 9 and it must NOT be equal to 9 for the statement to be true.

A student is writing a program that will search data to find suitable restaurants. The cost of the meal should be between £10 and £20. The type of food should be European or Asian and the restaurant should be no more than 10 miles away.

Complete the following algorithm by inserting the missing line.

```
cost = input("Please enter the cost of a meal.")
type = input("Please enter the type of food served.")
distance = input("Please enter the distance away of the restaurant".)

.........................................................................
   print("This restaurant is suitable.")
else
   print("This restaurant is not suitable.")
endif                            (3 marks)
```

# Selection

There are three basic programming constructs used to control program flow – sequence, selection and iteration.

**Sequence** ensures that the commands are executed in the correct order.

**Selection** is used in an algorithm to **choose between two or more options**. Selection involves the use of combinations of if, else and elseif statements in algorithms to choose between options.

## if/else

If/else statements can be used if there are only two possible outcomes.

If there are more than two outcomes, then it is not efficient to keep repeating them as each one is checked even after the selection has been made.

Instead elseif statements are used. These are more efficient: as soon as the correct condition is found, none of the rest of the options is checked.

else statements are used to state what should happen if none of the options in the if or elseif statements are true.

**Nested** if statements are if statements that are completely within another if statement.

Every if statement always needs its own endif statement.

The following example shows if …, elseif … and else … statements used for answering a multiple choice question.

```
answer = input("Please enter your choice")
if answer == "A" OR answer == "B" then
  print("Sorry, that is incorrect.")
elseif answer == "C" then
  print("Well done, that is correct.")
else
  print("That is not recognised.")
endif
```

The else statement is used to trap errors. It provides feedback if one of the expected values is not input.

## Switch/case

The **switch/case** construct can also be used for selection.

```
answer = input("Please enter your choice.")
switch answer:
  case "A":
    print("Sorry, that is incorrect.")
  case "B":
    print("Sorry, that is incorrect.")
  case "C":
    print("Well done, that is correct.")
  default:
    print("That is not recognised.")
endswitch
```

Here, the default statement is used to trap errors. It works in the same way as the else statement in the if…elseif….else construct.

**Worked example**

A bowling alley gives a 5% reduction in charge if there are four or more people on a lane and a further 10% reduction if they are members. Write the code that will calculate the final charge. **(5 marks)**

```
if numberOfPeople >= 4 then
  charge = charge - (charge/100*5)
  if membership == "Yes" then
    charge = charge -
    (charge/100*10)
  endif
endif
print("The charge is: " + charge)
```

**Now try this**

A shop gives a discount of 10% for purchases of £200 and over, up to a total discount of £300. Write an algorithm, in pseudocode, that would allow a user to calculate the discount. **(4 marks)**

# Iteration

Iteration is the process of repeating a set of instructions for a fixed number of times or until there is a desired outcome. It is executed by program constructs called loops.

## Count controlled iteration

**Count controlled** iteration is used when the number of iterations is known before the loop is started.

### for loops

for loops instruct the loop to be executed **for** a set number of times e.g.

```
for turns = 0 to 3
   print(turns)
next turns
```

This would output 0, 1, 2, 3

### while loops

Count controlled iteration can also be accomplished using while loops. The example above would be coded as:

```
turns = 0
while turns <= 3
   print(turns)
   turns = turns +1
endwhile
```

More lines of code are needed for the while loop and so it is less efficient than the for loop.

In the while loop the variable to be tested must be declared and given a value (initialised) before the loop is started. It must also be incremented or decremented each time the loop is run.

## Condition controlled iteration

**Condition controlled** iteration is used when the number of times a loop is executed is determined by a condition.

### while loops

while loops continue while a condition remains true and stop when it becomes false.

```
number = 0
while number != 3
   number = input("Please enter a number")
endwhile
```

The loop will continue while number does not equal 3. As soon as the number is equal to 3, the condition becomes false and the loop will stop.

### do...until loops

do ... until loops continue until a condition becomes true.

```
do
   number = input("Please enter a number")
until number == 3
```

In a while loop the condition is tested at the start of the loop but in a do ... until loop it is tested at the end and will therefore run at least once.

## Worked example

Write an algorithm in pseudocode that will print out a times table for any number entered by a user. The table should run from times 1 to 12. **(4 marks)**

```
number = input("Please enter a number.")
for times = 1 to 12
   print(number + "x" + times   "="   +
   number*times")
next times
```

In the print statement, variables and text have been **concatenated** (combined). They are joined by the '+' symbol and the text to be printed is enclosed in speech marks. Both while and do ... until loops could have been used in the answer but the for loop is far more efficient in this situation.

## Now try this

Write an algorithm in pseudocode for a game that will generate a random number between 1 and 10 for a user to guess. The user has three guesses. If they guess correctly they are told they are correct. If they do not guess correctly, they are told the randomly generated number. **(6 marks)**

# Data types

Computers must be aware of the **data type of values** stored in **variables** so that data is interpreted and manipulated correctly.

## Examples of data types

| Data type | Explanation | Example |
|---|---|---|
| Integer | An integer is a number without a fraction or decimal. Integers can be positive or negative. | 0, 3, 9, 100, 10 369 |
| Real | Real numbers include all numbers that exist and their fractions and decimals. Integers are real numbers. It is more efficient to declare integers as integers so that less memory is needed. In the OCR pseudocode, real numbers are declared as 'float'. | 2, 3.9, 6.632, 9.373 52 <br><br> float("1.25") |
| Boolean | A Boolean variable can have one of only two values – true or false. | reply = false <br> if answer == "y" or answer == "n" then <br>   reply = true <br> endif |
| Character | A character data type can store a single letter, number or symbol. | C <br> 3 <br> ! |
| String | A string can hold a list of characters of any length. When entered, they are enclosed in single or double quotation marks. | myString = "Hello user3 your password is ?!pass69Word" |

## Importance of data type

Data used by a computer are presented in strings of 1s and 0s. If the computer is not told the data type then it will not be able to use it correctly, e.g. it may try to multiply text and display numbers as images!

## Declaring data type

In some programming languages, the type must be declared; int age would declare that the variable "age" is to store integer numbers. In other languages, the type does not have to be stated. The type is inferred from the type of data first stored, e.g. age = 13 would imply that the variable age stores integers.

## Casting

**Casting** is the conversion of one data type into another, e.g. str(integerVariable) would convert an integer into a string. This must be done in some languages when concatenating variables and text in a print statement. int(stringVariable) or float(stringVariable) would convert a string into an integer or a real number.

### Worked example

Identify a data type that would be suitable for the variable 'response' in the following situations and state why it is the most appropriate.

(a) response = 10/7    **(2 marks)**

Real or float. It contains fractions or decimals.

(b) response = input("Please enter your name.")    **(2 marks)**

String. A person's name consists of a sequence of characters.

(c) response = input("Please enter your age in years.")    **(2 marks)**

Integer. It is a whole number without fractions or decimals.

### Now try this

State what is returned by each of the following statements:

• str(9)   • int(999)   • float(90)    **(3 marks)**

# String manipulation

A string is a sequence of characters that can contain letters, numbers and symbols.

## Strings

A **string literal** consists of characters enclosed in quotation marks, such as "A13!"

A **string variable** can be declared, such as

```
password = "A13!"
```

The same output can be obtained with different commands:

```
print("A13!")
```
——This is the **literal** string

```
print(password)
```
—— This is the **variable** string.

The two commands would produce the same output. The variable "password" is a string variable and it has a value of "A13!".

## Concatenation

Strings can be joined (concatenated) end to end to form larger strings using the + symbol.

```
firstName = "Jack"
lastName = "Jackson"
fullName = firstName + " " + lastName
```

A space " " has also been included in the concatenation so that there is a space between the two strings.
i.e. Jack Jackson instead of JackJackson.

## Indexes of a string

The position of a character in a string is given by its **index number**. The first index is 0, not 1.

| 0 | 1 | 2 | 3 | 4 | 5 |
|---|---|---|---|---|---|
| S | t | r | i | n | g |

In this string, the index of the character "i" is 3.

## String traversal

String traversal is the process of moving through a string one character at a time. It can be used to see if it contains a particular character or group of characters.

The **length** of the string must be found in order to create a **loop** to examine each character:

```
stringLength = myString.length
```

A loop can be set up to move through the string:

```
for index = 0 to stringLength -1
    character = myString(index)
    print(character)
next index
```

The loop must be set up to run from 0 to the length of the string **minus one** e.g. the string "Rosie and Jack" has a length of 14, so the indices are 0 to 13 (remember the spaces).
If the line in the code was

```
for index = 0 to stringLength
```

there would be an error message as there is not an index 14.

## Substrings

Substrings or portions of a string can be snipped out.

```
myString = "RosieandJack"
snip = myString.substring(2, 4)
print(snip)
```

The first number is the starting point and the second number is the number of characters.
This would print the word 'siea' as the substring starts at index 2 (the letter 's') and has a length of 4 characters.

### Worked example

A student has stored their computer science grades in a string variable named 'grades' e.g. 'AcBCab'. Write an algorithm, using pseudocode, that would count the number of occurrences of a grade entered by the user. **(5 marks)**

```
total = 0
searchGrade = input("Please enter
the grade.")
for index = 0 to grades.length - 1
if searchGrade.upper ==
grades(index).upper then
    total = total + 1
endif
next index
print("There are " + total + " "
searchGrade + " grades."
```

Both the grade entered by the user and the grade in the string have been converted to upper case for the comparison, as an upper case 'A' would not be equal to a lower case 'a'.

### Now try this

State the substring that would be printed by the following algorithm.

```
myString = "Computer Science"
substring = myString.substring(11, 3)
print(substring)
```
**(1 mark)**

# Arrays

Variables store one item of data that can change. Arrays are similar, but they can store multiple items of data, not just one.

## Arrays

An array is a data structure that can store multiple items of data, called **elements**, which are all of the **same data type under the same identifier**.

An array is created by specifying the elements stored in the array. This is called **declaring** the array. To store five players and their scores in separate arrays, you might declare the array like this:

```
array names = ["Alice", "Catherine",
"David", "Matthew", "Stephen"]
array scores = [10, 13, 17, 20, 3]
```

The elements in an array are enclosed within square brackets [   ] and are separated by commas.

## Two-dimensional arrays

In a two-dimensional (2D) array there is a second array at each index position of a one-dimensional (1D) array. This array of arrays forms a **matrix**. Each element has two indices to indicate its position, as shown in the table.

| 0, 0 | 0, 1 | 0, 2 | 0, 3 |
|------|------|------|------|
| 1, 0 | 1, 1 | 1, 2 | 1, 3 |
| 2, 0 | 2, 1 | 2, 2 | 2, 3 |
| 3, 0 | 3, 1 | 3, 2 | 3, 3 |
| 4, 0 | 4, 1 | 4, 2 | 4, 3 |

Original 1D array — Each data element has two indices to indicate its position. The two indices describe the **index position**.

An array with the structure as shown would be declared as `array arrayName [5, 4]`
This is because there are 5 indexes in the original array, and now 4 items of data in each position. For each of the elements 0 to 4, there are four items of data, 0 to 3.
Data can be assigned to an element using the index position:

```
array scores [5, 4]
scores [3, 3] = 15
```

## Indexes

An element is an item of data at a particular index.

| index | 0 | 1 | 2 | 3 | 4 |
|-------|---|---|---|---|---|
| element | red | green | blue | pink | brown |

The length of this array is 5 and the elements are at index positions 0 to 4.

The code to traverse this array would be:

```
for index = 0 to array.length - 1
  print(array[index])
next index
```

This code assumes the existence of a .length method for arrays that returns the length of an array.

### Worked example

A student recorded their resting pulse rate three times a day (8am, 12.30pm and 8pm) for four days and stored the data in a 2D array.

|            | 0  | 1  | 2  |
|------------|----|----|----|
| 0 (Day 1)  | 65 | 73 | 70 |
| 1 (Day 2)  | 69 | 75 | 68 |
| 2 (Day 3)  | 70 | 80 | 65 |
| 3 (Day 4)  | 68 | 79 | 69 |

(a) To output the pulse rate at noon on day 1 the student wrote the following code:

```
print(pulse[0, 1])
```

(i) State the pulse rate output from this statement. **(1 mark)**

73

(ii) Write the code to output the pulse rate in the evening on day 3. **(1 mark)**

```
print(pulse[2 2])
```

(b) Write the code that would output the average pulse rate for each day. **(5 marks)**

```
for day = 0 to 3
  total = 0
  for time = 0 to 2
    total = total + pulse[day, time]
  next time
  print("Average = " + total/3)
next day
```

### Now try this

A student has stored the first name and surname of each of their friends (in that order) into a 2D array named 'friends'. Write an algorithm that would allow the student to enter a friend's name and check whether that friend is in the array. **(5 marks)**

# File handling operations

Programming languages allow users to store data in files on storage devices so that they are not lost when a program is closed.

## Writing to a text file

**1** Before a file can be accessed or opened, it must be given a **file handle**. A file handle is a reference assigned to the file so that the program can access it. To do this using OCR pseudocode the following command is used:

```
myFile = openWrite("Sample.txt")
```

Here, myFile is the file handle.
"Sample.txt" is the name of the text file

**2** When a file is opened in **write** mode, a new file will be created with that filename if it does not already exist.

**3** If a file with that file name already exists, then it will be **overwritten** and the existing data will be lost. Most languages have an OpenAppend("Sample.txt") command to prevent this.

**4** Once a file has been read from or written to, it must be closed, e.g.

```
myFile.close()
```

## Writing directly

A user can open a file and write data directly to it from the keyboard.

```
myFile = openWrite("SampleFile.txt")
myFile.writeLine("My first name is
Fred.")
myFile.writeLine("My surname is
Smith.")
myFile.close()
```

The text file would have two lines of data.

## Writing indirectly

A program can be coded to save data stored in variables to a text file, e.g. the following data are stored in an array.

```
scoreFile = OpenWrite("highScores.txt")
array highScores = [10, 17, 13, 20, 15]
for index = 0 to highScores.length - 1
  scoreFile.writeLine(highScores[index])
next index
scoreFile.close()
```

Please see page 59 for more on arrays.

## Reading data from a file

A program can open a text file to read data.

```
myFile = openRead("Sample.txt")
```

The file name must always be in speech marks.

### Worked example

A student has coded a program that allows users to answer a multiple choice test. The user's name is stored in the 'userName' variable and their score in the 'testScore' variable.

Insert the code that would allow the score to be saved in a text file with the user's name in the filename. **(4 marks)**

```
userFile = openWrite(username + ".txt")
userFile.writeLine(testScore)
userFile.close()
```

## Reading

Data stored in a text file can be loaded into the variables of a program.

```
scoreFile = openRead("highScores.txt")
for index = 0 to 4
  highScores[index] = scoreFile.
  readLine()
next index
scoreFile.close()
```

The loop runs from 0 to 4 as there are 5 items to read in from the file.

If the number to read in is not known, the endOfFile() function can be used.

```
scoreFile = openRead("highScores.txt")
while NOT scoreFile.endOfFile()
  highScores[index] = scoreFile.
  readLine()
endwhile
scoreFile.close()
```

### Now try this

When using a program, a user is asked to create a username. Write a program that will ask a user to enter a username and check to see if it has already been used. Usernames are stored in a text file named 'users'.

If it has already been used, the routine should inform the user and ask them to enter a new one. **(8 marks)**

# Records

A record is a collection of data objects relating to a particular subject or entity. The data items stored in each record can be of **different data types**, e.g. integers and strings.

## Databases

Large volumes of data are usually stored in databases created using a database management system (DBMS). The data is stored in **tables** such as the one below. Each column heading defines a **field** (e.g. StudentNo, FirstName).

| StudentNo | FirstName | Surname | DOB | TutorGroup |
|-----------|-----------|---------|-----|------------|
| 001123 | Fred | Smith | 28/01/2001 | 10X |
| 001142 | Angela | Smith | 13/10/2000 | 10Y |
| 002567 | Mary | Green | 15/2/2001 | 10X |

Each record must have a **key field** that is an item of data that is **unique to that record**. In this table, it is the student number.

Each row is a **record** storing items of data about each individual student.

Each column is a **field** – an item of data stored in each record.

## Records in programming languages

Some programming languages allow users to create a data structure similar to that used in databases where the items of data can be of different data types. The records are often referred to as 'structs'. When these are set up, the data type for each element is usually stipulated as the elements, unlike those stored in arrays, can be of different data types.

## Creating records

In the C programming languages, a record structure similar to the database one above would be created in the following way.

```
struct student {
int StudentNo;
char FirstName[25];
char Surname[25];
int DOB;
char TutorGroup[3]
};
```

All the fields have been declared, their data types have been given and the maximum lengths of text fields specified.

### Worked example

A student is creating a database to store their music collection. They have identified the following fields: Name of artist(s), Name of song, Length of song, Date of release.

(a) Explain why none of the fields identified could be used as a key field. **(2 marks)**

A key field must contain unique data in each record. All of the fields identified could contain data found in other records.

(b) Suggest a suitable key field for the table. **(2 marks)**

A new field such as SongNumber could be created and a unique number inserted for each song.

### Now try this

Explain what is meant by the following terms:
- record
- field
- key field. **(6 marks)**

# Structured query language

Structured query language (SQL) is used for creating, maintaining and accessing databases. It allows users to search for records that contain a particular item or items of data. The examples used on this page refer to the database table on the previous page.

## SQL commands

For the examination, you will be expected to be able to use the following:

| SELECT | FROM |
|--------|------|
| WHERE  | LIKE |
| AND    | OR   |

## Searching with SQL

The **WHERE** keyword is used for searching.

```
SELECT FirstName, Surname
FROM Students
WHERE TutorGroup = "10X" AND DOB >
31/1/2001;
```

This would display first name and surname of Mary Green.

This would display the first name and surname of all three of the students.

```
SELECT FirstName, Surname
FROM Students
WHERE TutorGroup = "10X" OR
TutorGroup = "10Y";
```

Write commands on separate lines to make them easier to understand.

## Displaying records with SQL

The **SELECT** keyword is used to display records. Commands are **not** case sensitive – both SELECT and select will work.

```
SELECT * FROM Students;
```

This displays all the records and shows all their fields.

The * symbol is a wildcard and stands for 'show all fields'.

```
SELECT FirstName, Surname FROM
Students;
```

Notice the syntax – there is a semi-colon (;) at the end of a command.

This would display just those two fields for all the records.

### Wildcards

- ✓ The % symbol can be used as a substitute for one or many characters.
- ✓ The * symbol can be used to represent 'all fields', for example

```
WHERE TutorGroup LIKE "%X";
```

would return all records with a tutor group ending with an X, e.g. 7X, 9X, 10X etc.

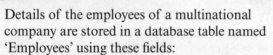

## Worked example

Details of the employees of a multinational company are stored in a database table named 'Employees' using these fields:
EmployeeNo, FirstName, Surname, DOB, Country, JobFunction.
Write the SQL commands that would return the following records.

- All employees showing only the Surname and Country fields.

```
SELECT Surname, Country FROM
Employees;
```

- Employees with the word 'computer' in their job titles. All fields should be displayed.   **(4 marks)**

```
SELECT * FROM Employees
WHERE JobFunction LIKE "%computer%";
```

## Now try this

Details of a school's students are stored in a database named 'Students' containing the following fields:

FirstName, Surname, DOB, Gender, Address1, Address2, Town, PostCode, SchoolYear, TutorGroup.

Write the SQL commands that would return the following records.

- All students showing the FirstName, Surname and PostCode fields.

- Students who are in the year 10 tutor group named East showing all the fields.   **(5 marks)**

# Sub-programs 1

A sub-program is a self-contained sequence of progam instructions that performs a specific task. Using sub-programs allows the production of more efficient code. A sub-program is called whenever it is needed to carry out that function. Sub-programs are also called subroutines.

## The uses of sub-programs

They:

- allow the production of structured code
- make programs shorter – the code only needs to be written once and can be called as many times as needed
- make program code easier to read and test
- shorten the development time of a program
- make testing easier
- make code more readable.

## Types of sub-programs

- ✓ A **function** is a sub-program that **returns a value** to the main program when it is called.
- ✓ A **procedure** is a sub-program that carries out a specific task but does not return values to the main program.
- ✓ Values passed to the function from the main program are stored in the sub-program's **parameters**.

Sub-programs need to be defined, e.g.

```
function functionName(parameters)
   code
   return
end function
```

or

```
procedure procedureName(parameters)
   code
endprocedure
```

## Creating a sub-program

The following code shows a function to calculate the velocity of an object.

To create a sub-program, you need to define it with its type, and indicate where it ends.

'velocity' is called a local variable as it is used only within the sub-program and not in the main program.

```
function vspeed(distance, time)
   velocity = distance/time
   return velocity
endfunction
```

You need to state the parameters that store the values that the function will use. These values are passed to them by the main program when the function is called.

The result of the calculation is returned to the main program.

## Worked example

The following program includes a sub-program. The lines have been numbered to assist you with the question.

```
1
2   print("Hello " + first + " " +
    last)
3
// The following is the main program
4 name1 = input("Enter first name.")
5 name2 = (input("Enter surname")
6 salutation(name1, name2)
```

(a) Complete the program by writing the code for:
  (i) line 1          **(2 marks)**
```
procedure salutation(first, last)
```
  (ii) line 3.          **(1 mark)**
```
endprocedure
```

(b) State **one** parameter used in the program.          **(1 mark)**
```
first or last
```

## Now try this

Write a sub-program that takes in a sentence entered by the user and returns the number of characters excluding spaces.          **(5 marks)**

# Sub-programs 2

Sub-programs can be called from within the main program.

## Calling a sub-program

```
function vspeed(distance, time)
  velocity = distance/time
  return velocity
endfunction

// main program
distanceTravelled = input("Please enter distance travelled in metres.")
timeTaken = input("Please enter time taken in seconds.")
averageVelocity = vspeed(distanceTravelled, timeTaken)
print(averageVelocity)
```

"velocity" is a local variable. It only exists within the sub-program.

The calculation is performed and the local variable velocity is passed back to the global variable averageVelocity in the main program.

This is the main program that calls the function.

This line **calls** the function and passes the values of two **global variables** to it as **arguments** in the **correct order**. In the sub-program, these values are passed into the parameters 'distance' and 'time' above.

It's best not to use the same names for local and global variables because then you could get into a muddle with the logic and mix them up.

These are **global variables**. They exist within the main program and can be referenced in other lines of code.

## Procedures

**Procedures** do not return a value to the main program. They could print out a message for the user, e.g.

```
procedure printMessage(first, second)
    print ("Hello " + first   + " " +
    second + ".")
endprocedure
```

The procedure on the left has two parameters – 'first' and 'second'– that are passed to it from the main program:

```
firstName = input("Enter first name.")
secondName = input("Enter second name.")
printMessage(firstName, secondName)
```

---

**Worked example**

The following is part of a program and a function to return the area of a rectangle.

```
function rectangle (length, width)
  area = length * width
  return area
endfunction
// main program
rectArea = rectangle(rectLength, rectWidth)
print(rectArea)
```

(a) List **two** global variables.          (2 marks)

Any two of rectArea, rectLength, rectWidth

(b) List **two** parameters.          (2 marks)

length, width

(c) State a local variable.          (1 mark)

area

---

**Now try this**

A student is creating a computer version of a board game during which each user has to shake two dice and find the total.

Create a function that will simulate the dice throws and return the total to the main program.          (4 marks)

# Defensive design

Computer programs should be designed to ensure that they can cope with unexpected or erroneous input from users.

## Why defensive design is important

Defensive design ensures that:

- the number of errors or bugs is minimised
- the program behaves as expected in spite of unexpected user actions
- all possible errors that could occur are identified and allowed for.

Computer scientists should plan for all contingencies that might occur. These include accidental or deliberate erroneous inputs or item selections.

## Authentication

✓ Authentication is the process of determining the identity of a user.

✓ Authentication is usually based on a **username** and an associated **password**.

✓ Authentication checks that the username and password exist.

Take care – even if the username and its password are correct, it does not prove that the person inputting them is the person to whom they were issued. It may be identity theft!

## Validation

The validation process checks that data that is input is sensible, reasonable and appropriate to be processed by the program. These checks should be used to ensure that required data is actually input and is within a certain range or of a required length. Some common validation techniques include:

### ① Presence check

Presence checks ensure that data has been entered.

```
entry = ""
while entry == ""
  entry = input("Please enter the
  text.")
  if entry == "" then
    print("No entry has been made.")
  endif
endwhile
```

### ③ Length check

Length checks ensure that a specified number of characters have been entered.

```
password = ""
while password == ""
  password = input("Please enter the
  password.")
  if password.length < 8 then
    print("Not long enough.")
    password = ""
  endif
endwhile
```

### ② Range check

Range checks ensure that an input falls within a required range.

```
entry = 0
  while entry == 0
  input("Please enter the number.")
  if number < 10 OR number > 20 then
    print("Please enter a number
    between 10 and 20.")
    number = 0
  endif
endwhile
```

### Worked example

(a) Define what is meant by validation. **(1 mark)**
Validation is the process of checking that any data that is input is sensible, reasonable and appropriate.

(b) State what is meant by a presence check. **(1 mark)**

A presence check ensures that some data has in fact been input.

(c) State what is meant by a range check. **(1 mark)**
A range check ensures that the data entered fall within a certain range of values.

## Now try this

Write an algorithm, using pseudocode, that allows a user to enter the month and day of their birth as a number. Your algorithm should have routines to validate each entry. **(8 marks)**

# Testing and maintainability

Testing ensures that the software produces the expected results and meets the needs of the users.

## Testing

1. All software should be tested to ensure that it is **robust** so it produces the expected results and can withstand malicious users.

2. Testing should be **destructive** and should try to find errors rather than just proving that a program works.

3. Tests are often done at two points in the software design and development:
   - **Iterative tests** are carried out as the software is being developed. Tests are carried out on each module and the results are used to inform further development.
   - **Final** or **terminal testing** is carried out once the software has been developed. **Alpha testing** is done by the developers and then **beta testing** by potential users of the software.

## Suitable test data

Suitable test data must be used to test the software in all situations.

1. **Normal data** tests the software under normal working conditions.

2. **Boundary data** tests the software under extreme conditions, e.g. it will test that length and range checks are functioning correctly.

3. **Erroneous data** tests how the software deals with incorrect inputs that may be entered deliberately or by mistake. The program should have routines to deal with them and inform the user that data is, for example, outside an expected range or numbers are entered instead of text.

## Syntax and logical errors

1. **Syntax errors** are grammatical mistakes in code, which could be caused by a misspelling, (prnit instead of print) or by missing colons, semi-colons or brackets. Syntax errors will prevent a program from running and are difficult to spot. They can be prevented by using an **IDE** – integrated development environment.

You can read more about IDEs on page 71.

2. **Logic errors** cause unintended output because of a fault in the logic of the algorithm e.g. using the AND operator instead of the OR operator, or a loop that may run forever. Trace tables help to identify logic errors.

## Maintainability

☑ Program code should be easy to follow and understand in case changes have to be made or errors corrected.

☑ Explanations should be added to explain the code. **Comments** are shown using two forward slashes (//).

☑ All code that depends on a previous statement should be **indented** e.g.

```
for index = 0 to 9
   print(index)
endfor
```

☑ It is easier to follow and understand a program when **meaningful identifiers** have been used.

## Worked example

The following statement is part of a program for entering student data into a school system:

```
if yearGroup < 7 OR yearGroup > 13
then
   print("Incorrect entry.")
endif
```

Suggest suitable data that could be used for the following tests.

- Boundary test                                    **(1 mark)**

7

- Erroneous data                                   **(1 mark)**

100

For the first part 13 could also have been entered as boundary data.

For the second part any number **other than** 7, 8, 9, 10, 11, 12, 13 could be entered.

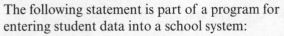

## Now try this

1. Explain the difference between a syntax error and a logic error.                    **(2 marks)**

2. Describe **two** techniques that computer scientists use to make their programs easier to read, understand and maintain.          **(4 marks)**

# Computational logic 1

In computational logic, all possible outcomes are either **TRUE** or **FALSE**. This is important for computers because computers can also only have two states – **on** and **off** – represented by 1 and 0 in binary.

## Boolean logic and computers

Boolean logic is a form of algebra in which all values are reduced to one of two states, TRUE or FALSE. Boolean logic is especially important for computer science as it fits with the binary system in which each bit has a value of either 1 or 0, that is, each bit has a value of either TRUE or FALSE.

## Transistors

A processor contains over 1 billion transistors. The transistors either transmit an electric current (on) or they do not (off). These two states of on or off can be used to represent the two conditions of true (on) or false (off).

A transistor

## Logic gates

Logic gates use transistors that carry out all of the calculations and execute program instructions in the processor. Logic gates are represented by symbols in logic diagrams.

| AND gate | OR gate | NOT gate |
|---|---|---|
| A —⊐& ⊐— Q  B —  | A —⊐≥1 ⊐— Q  B —  | A —▷o— Q |
| For an output at Q there must be an input at both A **AND** B. | For an output at Q there must be an input at either one of A **OR** B or at **both of them**. | There is an output at Q only if there is **NOT** an input at A. |

Go back to page 54 for more about the Boolean operators AND, OR and NOT and about combining the operations.

## Truth tables

The states of the inputs and outputs of the gates can be shown using truth tables where a 1 or a 0 is used to indicate the presence or absence of an electric current.

| AND gate | | | | OR gate | | | | NOT gate | |
|---|---|---|---|---|---|---|---|---|---|
| **A** | **B** | **Q** | | **A** | **B** | **Q** | | **A** | **Q** |
| 0 | 0 | 0 | | 0 | 0 | 0 | | 0 | 1 |
| 0 | 1 | 0 | | 0 | 1 | 1 | | 1 | 0 |
| 1 | 0 | 0 | | 1 | 0 | 1 | | | |
| 1 | 1 | 1 | | 1 | 1 | 1 | | | |

AND gate: There is an output at Q only if there are inputs at A **AND** B.

OR gate: There is an output at Q if there is an input at A **OR** B or at both of them.

NOT gate: There is an output at Q only if there is **NOT** an input at A.

Complete the following logic diagrams by filling in the blanks with 0 or 1.     **(2 marks)**

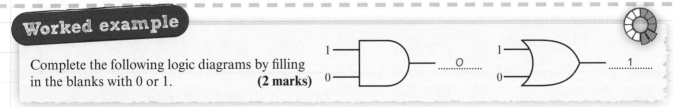

1 —⊐& ⊐..0.. 1 —⊐≥1 ⊐..1..
0 —      0 —

Copy and complete the logic diagram by filling in the blanks with 0 or 1.     **(1 mark)**

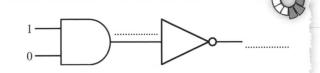

1 —⊐& ⊐........ ▷o— ........
0 —

# Computational logic 2

Logic diagrams and truth tables can be used to solve logic problems.

## Boolean statements

The Boolean statement **P = A AND B** implies that P is true only if both A and B are true. It can be investigated using a truth table.

| A | B | P |
|---|---|---|
| FALSE | FALSE | FALSE |
| FALSE | TRUE | FALSE |
| TRUE | FALSE | FALSE |
| TRUE | TRUE | TRUE |

The NOT statement reverses the logic so if A AND B are false then P is true.

**Worked example**

Complete the truth table below for the Boolean expression P = NOT(A AND B).     **(4 marks)**

| A | B | P |
|---|---|---|
| FALSE | FALSE | TRUE |
| FALSE | TRUE | TRUE |
| TRUE | FALSE | TRUE |
| TRUE | TRUE | FALSE |

## Using Boolean statements to solve problems

Boolean statements can be used to represent selection using relational operators used in programs. For example the statement

```
if X == 9 AND Y == 6 then
```

is the same as **P = A AND B** above.

The statement

```
if NOT(X == 9 AND Y == 6) then
```

is the same as

```
P = NOT(A AND B)
```

The statement

```
if X != 9 AND Y != 6 then
```

could be represented as the Boolean expression:
P = (NOT A) AND (NOT B)

**Worked example**

Complete the truth table below for the Boolean expression **P = (NOT A) AND (NOT B)**.     **(4 marks)**

| A | B | P |
|---|---|---|
| FALSE | FALSE | TRUE |
| FALSE | TRUE | FALSE |
| TRUE | FALSE | FALSE |
| TRUE | TRUE | FALSE |

P is true **only** when A is not true AND B is not true. It is different to the first worked example. Therefore the statement:
`if NOT (X == 9 AND Y == 6)` is **not** the same as `if (X !=9 AND Y != 6)`.

**Worked example**

Complete a logic diagram for the equation
P = NOT(A) AND B     **(2 marks)**

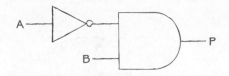

Complete the truth table for the logic circuit you have drawn.     **(3 marks)**

| A | B | P |
|---|---|---|
| 0 | 0 | 0 |
| 0 | 1 | 1 |
| 1 | 0 | 0 |
| 1 | 1 | 0 |

## Now try this

An alarm system uses three switches. The alarm will sound if either switch A or switch B are in the ON position but only if the master switch C is in the ON position.

Draw a logic diagram and truth table for this system.     **(5 marks)**

# Programming languages

Instructions for computers are written in programming languages that need to be translated into machine code before the computer can understand them.

## Levels of computer languages

| Low-level languages | | High level language |
|---|---|---|

### Machine language

Processors only understand instructions written in 1s and 0s. At the processing level, computer programs are in the form of millions of 1s and 0s. This is known as **machine code** or **machine language**. Machine code is a **low-level** language.

### Assembly language

Assembly language is a low-level language. Each instruction in assembly language is directly equivalent to one in machine code. Words called **mnemonics** are used to replace the command represented as strings of 1s and 0s in machine code, e.g. ADD is a mnemonic used to replace the binary command to add number together.

### High level language

High-level languages are programming languages that resemble human languages. They use key words such as 'print', 'if' and 'then'. High-level languages address the programming logic rather than dealing with hardware issues such as memory addressing. Most programs are written in high-level languages.

## Use of low-level languages

✓ Assembly language is often used in the programs used by embedded systems such as those in cameras, microwaves and televisions as it can be used to directly control system hardware.

✓ They are used to write device drivers and real-time systems where speed is essential.

✓ Assembly language is specific to each type of CPU. Programs written for one type cannot be used on others.

## Use of high-level languages

✓ Most software is developed using a high-level language. It is less time-consuming to write and quicker to test.

✓ Programs are portable from one machine to another.

✓ Most high-level languages can be used with different types of CPU.

See page 6 for more on embedded systems.

## Worked example

A program is being developed using a high-level programming language.

(a) Explain what is meant by a high-level programming language. **(2 marks)**

A high-level programming language is similar to a natural human language. It uses key words such as 'print', 'if' and 'then'. Programs written in a high-level language have to be translated into machine code to operate.

(b) State **two** advantages of using a high-level language for software development. **(2 marks)**

It is quicker to develop and test the software. The software will be able to run on computers with different types of processor.

You are asked to **explain** and a longer answer is required including two linked statements.

You are asked to **state** two advantages, so explanations of the statements are not required.

## Now try this

1 State what is meant by an embedded system. **(1 mark)**

2 Explain why assembly language is often used to write software for embedded systems. **(2 marks)**

# Translators

Programs written in assembly languages and high-level languages (**source code**) must be **translated into machine code** (object code) before the processor can execute them. **Compilers** and **interpreters** are examples of translators.

## Compiler

A **compiler** translates the source code into a standalone, machine code program (object code) that can then be executed by the processor.

👍 The translation is done once only and as a separate process.

👍 The program that is run is already translated into machine code so it can be executed more rapidly.

👍 It protects the software from competitors who would otherwise be able to see the source code.

👎 If it encounters any errors, it carries on trying to compile the program and reports the errors at the end. The programmers then have to use the error messages to identify and remove the bugs.

You cannot change the program without going back to the original source code, editing that and recompiling.

## Interpreter

An **interpreter** translates the high-level code line by line into machine code. It is needed each time the program is run.

👍 When an error is found, the interpreter reports it and stops and pinpoints the error so that the programmer knows where it has occurred.

👍 The code is not platform specific and can be run on different operating systems and platforms as long as there is an interpreter.

👍 The program can be easily edited as it always exists as source code.

👎 Every line has to be translated every time it is executed and therefore it is slower to run.

## Assemblers

**Assemblers** translate the **mnemonics of assembly language** into machine code instructions. Assembly language is very similar to machine code. There is one assembly language instruction for each machine language instruction.

---

## Worked example

(a) Explain why program code developed using a high-level language must be translated.

**(2 marks)**

Instructions must be translated into machine code as that is the only language that the processor can execute.

(b) A compiler or an interpreter can be used to translate the code.

State **one** advantage and **one** disadvantage of using each of these translators. **(4 marks)**

An advantage of using an interpreter is that it will stop when it finds an error and will pinpoint the error for the developer.

A disadvantage of using an interpreter is that it is slower to execute the program as each line must be translated each time it is run.

An advantage of using a compiler is that the translation needs to be done only once.

A disadvantage of using a compiler is that if the program needs to be changed, then the original source code has to be edited and recompiled.

---

## Now try this

Compare the methods used by compilers and interpreters to translate high-level code into machine code.

**(2 marks)**

# Integrated development environment

An integrated development environment (IDE) provides facilities for computer programmers to develop software more efficiently.

## Source code editor

A source code editor is a text editor designed for writing and editing source code.

```
def getKey():
  kent=False
  while kent==False:
    try:
      key=int(input("Please enter a key:     "))
    except ValueError:
      print ("The key must be a number between 1 and 25.")
      continue
    if (key<26 and key>1):
        kent=True
    else:
        print("Please enter a key between 1 and 26.")
  return (key)
```

**Syntax highlighting** displays source code in different colours and fonts according to type, e.g. commands, variables, control statements and strings.

**Bracket matching** highlights matching sets of delimiters such as brackets or quote marks. It helps the programmer navigate through the code and spot any that do not match.

**Auto indentation** automatically indents the next line if it is required.

**Autocomplete** or **word completion** predicts a word or command that the user is typing and completes it.

## Error diagnostics

❶ Facilities are provided to debug the code. **Single-stepping** allows the code to be run and inspected one line at a time. It shows the result of a single command.

❷ **Breakpoints** allow the code to be stopped at selected positions. If there is a problem, then the programmer can set sequential breakpoints to see in which section the error occurs.

❸ **Variable tracing** allows the programmer to inspect the values of variables at any point in the program to check if they are as expected.

### Run-time environment

Run-time environment allows the code to run within the IDE as though it was actually running on the processor. This means that the programmer does not have to waste time preparing the program to run on the real CPU. In order for the code to run within the IDE, it has to go through a translator.

## Worked example

A student is using an integrated development environment (IDE) to write a program.

(a) State what is meant by an integrated development environment. **(1 mark)**

An IDE is a software application that provides facilities to computer programmers for software development.

(b) Describe **two** tools available in an IDE that help programmers to write and check code. **(1 mark)**

The code editor allows the programmer to write code more efficiently as it provides syntax highlighting and auto-indentation.

Error diagnostics help the programmer to identify errors by allowing the use of single-stepping and breakpoints.

## Now try this

Apart from a source code editor, state **two** other components you would expect to find in an IDE. **(2 marks)**

# Data representation

All data processed by a computer must be converted into binary format.

## Computers and binary

A computer processor uses billions of transistors acting as switches, which only act on the binary states on and off. All data and instructions are represented by the binary digits 1 (on) and 0 (off).

## Representation of data

To be processed, instructions and data are converted to strings of 1s and 0s. Images and sounds must be **digitised** and other inputs (keyboard and mouse) send combinations of 1s and 0s to the processor.

## Units

One unit, either a 1 or a 0, is called a **bit** – short for **binary digit**. More than one digit is needed to represent an item of data (such as a letter). Bits are organised into groups.

4 bits = 1 **nibble** and 8 bits = 1 **byte**. Bytes are grouped into the larger units shown below.

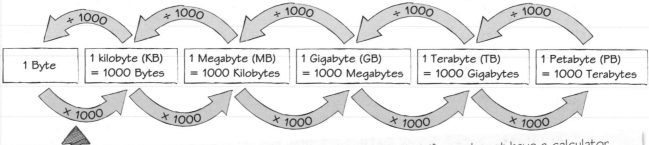

| ÷ 1000 | ÷ 1000 | ÷ 1000 | ÷ 1000 | ÷ 1000 |
|---|---|---|---|---|

| 1 Byte | 1 kilobyte (KB) = 1000 Bytes | 1 Megabyte (MB) = 1000 Kilobytes | 1 Gigabyte (GB) = 1000 Megabytes | 1 Terabyte (TB) = 1000 Gigabytes | 1 Petabyte (PB) = 1000 Terabytes |

| × 1000 | × 1000 | × 1000 | × 1000 | × 1000 |
|---|---|---|---|---|

The binary prefix 1024 may also be used in questions but if you do not have a calculator the decimal prefix 1000 is easier to use. The question should tell you which one you should use but if it doesn't it is perfectly correct to use 1000.

## Number systems

**1** The **binary** system is a **base-2** number system that uses two digits: 0 and 1.

**2** The **denary** system (often called the decimal system) is a **base-10** (**decimal**) number system that uses 10 digits: 0 to 9.

**3** The **hexadecimal** system is a **base-16** number system that uses 16 digits: 0 to 15.

## The values of the digits

In any system, the value associated with any digit is given by its **place value**. The value of each position increases as the power of its base. The table shows how this works for binary.

| Place value | $2^7$ | $2^6$ | $2^5$ | $2^4$ | $2^3$ | $2^2$ | $2^1$ | $2^0$ |
|---|---|---|---|---|---|---|---|---|
| Value | 128 | 64 | 32 | 16 | 8 | 4 | 2 | 1 |

Place value works in the same way for denary, with a base of 10. Denary numbers are the numbers we use in most of our everyday calculations.

| Place value | $10^7$ | $10^6$ | $10^5$ | $10^4$ | $10^3$ | $10^2$ | $10^1$ | $10^0$ |
|---|---|---|---|---|---|---|---|---|
| Value | 10 000 000 | 1 000 000 | 100 000 | 10 000 | 1000 | 100 | 10 | 1 |

The number 10 in binary has a very different value to 10 in denary. 10 in binary is 2 in denary.

## Worked example

An image file has a size of 57 600 000 bits.

Express this in megabytes. You may use the decimal prefix (1000) in your calculation. **(2 marks)**

57 600 000 bits ÷ 8 = 7 200 000 bytes

7 200 000 ÷ 1000 = 7200 kilobytes

7200 ÷ 1000 = 7.2 megabytes

## Now try this

Showing your working, express 1 petabyte in bits. You may use the decimal prefix (1000) in your calculation. **(2 marks)**

# Converting from denary to binary

You can convert **denary** numbers with values from 0 to 255 into **8 bit binary numbers**. Denary numbers above 255 require more bits. Denary numbers are also called **decimal** numbers.

Follow the steps in the flow chart to convert a denary number to a binary number.

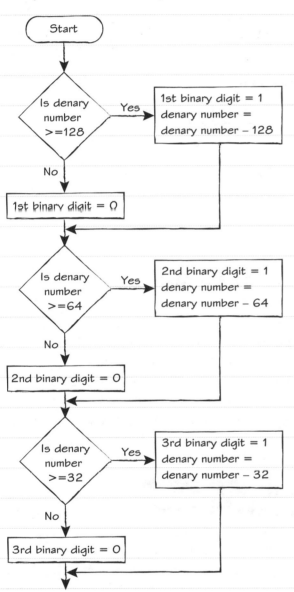

Continue this processing for the 4th to 8th binary digits using the values of $2^4$, $2^3$, $2^2$, $2^1$ and $2^0$.

## Worked example

Convert the denary number 217 into an 8 bit binary number. **(1 mark)**

| Compare | Binary digit | Next value |
|---------|--------------|------------|
| 217 > 128 | 1 | 217 – 128 = 89 |
| 89 > 64 | 1 | 89 – 64 = 25 |
| 25 < 32 | 0 | 25 |
| 25 > 16 | 1 | 25 – 16 = 9 |
| 9 > 8 | 1 | 9 – 8 = 1 |
| 1 < 4 | 0 | 1 |
| 1 < 2 | 0 | 1 |
| 1 ≥ 1 | 1 | |

The number is 11011001.

If the number is **larger** than the place value you are comparing, remember to **subtract** that place value to get your next starting value. Check that your final number has **8 binary digits**.

## Check your answers

You can check by converting your 8 bit binary number back into a denary number:

| 1 | 1 | 0 | 1 | 1 | 0 | 0 | 1 |
|---|---|---|---|---|---|---|---|
| $2^7$ | $2^6$ | $2^5$ | $2^4$ | $2^3$ | $2^2$ | $2^1$ | $2^0$ |
| 128 | 64 | 0 | 16 | 8 | 0 | 0 | 1 |

$128 + 64 + 0 + 16 + 8 + 0 + 0 + 1 = 217$

There is more about converting from binary to denary on page 74.

## Now try this

Convert the following denary numbers into 8 bit binary numbers:

- 203
- 241
- 79
- 100      **(4 marks)**

Watch out! If the denary number is less than 128 then the first binary digit will be 0. You have been asked to find an **8 bit** binary number, so you must include the initial 0.

# Converting from binary to denary and binary addition

Binary numbers can also be converted to denary numbers.

## Binary to denary

**1** Write down the place values up to $2^7$ from right to left.

**2** Write down their denary value.

**3** Write down the binary number in the correct position.

**4** Multiply the values to give the denary value for each binary digit.

**5** Add all the answers together to get the denary total.

All you have to remember are the place values and multiply each one by the digit at that place – either a 1 or a 0.

**Worked example**

Convert the binary number 11011001 into a denary (decimal) number. **(1 mark)**

| Place value | $2^7$ | $2^6$ | $2^5$ | $2^4$ | $2^3$ | $2^2$ | $2^1$ | $2^0$ |
|---|---|---|---|---|---|---|---|---|
| Denary value | 128 | 64 | 32 | 16 | 8 | 4 | 2 | 1 |
| Binary number | 1 | 1 | 0 | 1 | 1 | 0 | 0 | 1 |
| Denary | 128 | 64 | 0 | 16 | 8 | 0 | 0 | 1 |

$128 + 64 + 16 + 8 + 1 = 217$

11011001 in binary is equal to 217 in denary.

**Worked example**

Add together the following two 8 bit binary numbers: 00101011 + 00010111 **(1 mark)**

```
   0 0 1 0 1 0 1 1
 + 0 0 0 1 0 1 1 1
   0 1 0 0 0 0 1 0
     1 1 1 1 1 1
```

## Binary addition

Binary addition follows the same rules as denary.

**1** Write the numbers out one above the other, with an addition sign.

**2** Start at the right and add the numbers, remembering that this is binary.

**3** $1 + 0 = 1$, $0 + 0 = 0$ but $1 + 1 = 10$, so you need to write the 0 and carry the 1 to the left.

## Overflow errors

An **overflow error** occurs when a calculation produces a result that is greater than the computer can deal with, e.g.

```
  1 0 1 1 0 1 0 1
  1 1 0 0 1 1 1 1
1 1 0 0 0 0 1 0 0
```

The result cannot be represented by an 8 bit number. A **9th bit** is required – this is the overflow. Programmers must make allowances for this to prevent serious errors or disasters.

**Worked example**

(a) Add together the following two 8 bit binary numbers: 10010111 and 11011000.

Express your response in an 8 bit binary form. **(2 marks)**

```
   1 0 0 1 0 1 1 1
 + 1 1 0 1 1 0 0 0
 1 0 1 1 0 1 1 1 1
   1     1
```

(b) Identify the problem the addition has created. **(1 mark)**

There is an overflow error because the result cannot be represented in 8 bits.

**Now try this**

Convert the 8 bit binary number 10010111 into a decimal number. **(2 marks)**

Show the carry digits, identify the overflow, and explain why the overflow has occurred.

# Binary shifts

Binary shifts are used when multiplying or dividing binary numbers by powers of 2.

## Multiplying binary numbers by powers of 2

Binary shifts are the equivalent of multiplying denary numbers by a power of 10 and moving the digits to the **left** and writing zeros at the right-hand end. In denary, e.g.,
$22 \times 100 = 22 \times 10^2 = 2200$
A similar method works in **binary**, but with **multiplying by 2** or **powers of 2**.

- $\times 2^2$: shift 2 places to the left
- $\times 2^3$: shift 3 places to the left
- $\times 2^4$: shift 4 places to the left.

## Dividing binary numbers by powers of 2

When you **divide** binary numbers by powers of 2, you move bits to the right – **right shifts**.

### Worked example

Multiply 00011110 (30) by $2^2$.  **(1 mark)**

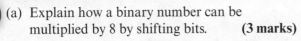

Answer: 01111000

Each digit moves 2 places to the left because the power is 2 and the number is being multiplied. Any spaces (on the right-hand side) that are created as a result of the left shift are filled with 0s.

**Check it!** Convert the binary number to denary to check your answer.
00011110 is 30 in denary.
$2^2$ is 4.
The answer should be $30 \times 4 = 120$.
$01111000 = 64 + 32 + 16 + 8 = 120$ ✓

### Worked example

(a) Explain how a binary number can be multiplied by 8 by shifting bits.  **(3 marks)**

8 is equal to $2^3$ so all the bits should be moved 3 places to the left. 0s should be inserted into the 3 rightmost positions.

(b) Complete a 3-place right shift on the binary number 10110100. Explain why there is a loss in precision.  **(2 marks)**

In denary, this would be $180 \div 8 = 22.5$
Performing the 3-place right shift:

| Original number | 1 | 0 | 1 | 1 | 0 | 1 | 0 | 0 |
|---|---|---|---|---|---|---|---|---|
| Result of right shifts | 0 | 0 | 0 | 1 | 0 | 1 | 1 | 0 |

Converting 00010110 to denary is 22, which is less than 22.5. This is because the answer is given as the nearest lower integer in a right binary shift, so some precision is lost.

In part (a), make sure you remember to explain where the bits should move, by how many places and why. You also need to explain where the 0s need to be inserted.
In part (b), it's worth noting that precision can also be lost when dividing denary numbers, for example, if you divide 201 by 10 by shifting bits along, with no decimal place, you get 20, not 20.1.

### Worked example

Divide 10111000 by $2^3$.  **(1 mark)**

Answer: 00010111

Each digit moves 3 places to the right because the power is 3 and the number is being divided. Any spaces (on the left-hand side) created as a result of the right shift are filled with 0s.

**Check it!**
10111000 is 184 in denary.
$2^3$ is 8.
$184 \div 8 = 23$.
Convert the binary number to its denary equivalent:
$00010111 = 16 + 4 + 2 + 1 = 23$ ✓

### Now try this

1  Complete a 2-place left shift on the binary number 00010100.  **(1 mark)**

2  Complete a 3-place right shift on the binary number 10001000.  **(1 mark)**

# Hexadecimal and denary

Hexadecimal is a base 16 number system.

## Hexadecimal

Hexadecimal numbers need 16 digits, but we have no denary digits beyond 9, so the denary numbers 10 to 15 are represented by **upper case** letters A to F.

Denary 0 1 2 3 4 5 6 7 8 9 10 11 12 13 14 15
Hex    0 1 2 3 4 5 6 7 8 9 A  B  C  D  E  F

The # symbol is used to signify that a number is given in hexadecimal notation.

### Place value

| Place values | $16^3$ | $16^2$ | $16^1$ | $16^0$ |
|---|---|---|---|---|
| Denary values | 4096 | 256 | 16 | 1 |

All denary numbers up to 255 can be represented by hexadecimal numbers with only two digits.

## Converting denary to hexadecimal

1. Write the number you are converting.

2. Divide it by 16.

3. Write the result and the remainder in their own columns.

4. Divide the result by 16 as in ②.

5. The numbers in the remainder column become the hexadecimal number. The second remainder is the first digit of the hexadecimal number.

### Worked example

Convert the denary number 230 into hexadecimal. **(1 mark)**

| Number | Divide by 16 | Remainder | Hex |
|---|---|---|---|
| 230 | 14 | 6 | 6 |
| 14 | 0 | 14 | E |

E6

The hexadecimal number is E6 as the number 14 is represented as the digit E.

### Worked example

Convert the following hexadecimal numbers into denary. **(2 marks)**

(a) CD

CD = (12 × 16) + 13 = 192 + 13 = 205

(b) 3F

3F = (3 × 16) + 15 = 48 + 15 = 63

## Converting hexadecimal to denary

1. Multiply the first digit by 16.

2. Add the second digit.

You do not have to do any multiplication for a 1-digit hexadecimal number. The denary number is the 1-digit hexadecimal number, e.g. A in hexadecimal = 10 in denary.

### Worked example

(a) Convert the denary (decimal) number 236 into a hexadecimal number. **(1 mark)**

236 ÷ 16 = 14, remainder = 12
14 ÷ 16 = 0, remainder = 14
Hexadecimal = EC

(b) Convert the hexadecimal number 9C into a denary (decimal) number. **(1 mark)**

9C = (9 × 16) + 12
   = 144 + 12 = 156

### Now try this

In a colour selector in a graphics program, the code for a 24-bit colour called Firebrick can be represented by the RGB code 178-34-34 consisting of three denary numbers.

How would the colour be represented in hexadecimal notation in the colour selector?

Explain your answer. **(3 marks)**

# Hexadecimal and binary

Hexadecimal numbers are used to help programmers manipulate large binary numbers because computers do not use hexadecimal numbers - they only understand binary. Hexadecimal numbers represent long binary numbers using fewer digits, as every eight digits of a binary number can be represented by two hexadecimal digits.

## Worked example

Convert the binary number 10110011 in to a hexadecimal number. **(2 marks)**

10110011

1011 →      ← 0011

place value →

| 1 | 0 | 1 | 1 |
|---|---|---|---|
| 8 | 4 | 2 | 1 |
| 8 | 0 | 2 | 1 |

= 8 + 2 + 1 = **11**

| 0 | 0 | 1 | 1 |
|---|---|---|---|
| 8 | 4 | 2 | 1 |
| 0 | 0 | 2 | 1 |

= 2 + 1 = **3**

11 in hexadecimal is B
3 in hexadecimal is 3

Therefore the hexadecimal number is **B3**

## Converting binary to hexadecimal

1. Split the **8 bit byte** into two **4-bit nibbles**.

2. Convert the bits in each nibble into denary numbers using the place values.

3. Add these together to give the hexadecimal.

## Converting hexadecimal to binary

Converting hexadecimal to binary reverses the process of converting binary to a hexadecimal number.

1. Each hexadecimal digit is converted to denary.
2. Each denary number is converted into a nibble.
3. The nibbles are combined to give the binary number.

## Worked example

Convert the hexadecimal C3 to binary. **(2 marks)**

C3

12 ←      → 3

| 8 | 4 | 2 | 1 |
|---|---|---|---|
| 1 | 1 | 0 | 0 |

| 8 | 4 | 2 | 1 |
|---|---|---|---|
| 0 | 0 | 1 | 1 |

→ 11000011

## Use of hexadecimal

☑ Hexadecimal notation is used to help humans cope with long strings of binary digits – they are much shorter in hexadecimal.

☑ MAC addresses are given in hexadecimal form.

☑ When a computer malfunctions, error code numbers are usually given in hexadecimal.

☑ Hexadecimal is also used to represent numerical values in assembly language.

See page 16 for more on MAC addresses.

## True colour

True colour uses 24 bits to code every available colour variation: $2^{24} = 16\,777\,216$. Each one is represented by three 8 bit numbers that can be simplified to three 2-digit hexadecimal ones, e.g. 110001100011000011110100 can be represented as C630F4. It is far easier to remember and enter the six digits of the hexadecimal number than the 24 digits of the binary number.

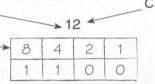

#FF0000   #FFA500   z      #00FF00   #00FFFF   #0000FF   #FF00FF

HEX

## Worked example

Convert the bit pattern 10110111 into hexadecimal. **(1 mark)**

1011 = 11 in denary
0111 = 7 in denary
= B7 in hexadecimal.

## Now try this

Convert the hexadecimal number E9 into a binary number. You must show your working. **(2 marks)**

# Check digits

**Check digits** are used to ensure that a sequence of numbers has been entered correctly. Errors made when entering data are called **transcription errors** and check digits are used to flag up these errors. Examples of codes that use check digits include product codes in shops and ISBNs on books.

## Calculating the modulus 11 check digit

It is called this as a MOD or modulus division by 11 is carried out to find the remainder.

1. If a code needs 8 digits, the first 7 are generated and then the 8th is calculated as the check digit.

2. The algorithm gives each digit a weighting, starting with 2, from right to left. The weighting is stipulated by the algorithm.

3. Multiply each digit by its weighting.

4. Add each subtotal to find the total.

5. Divide the total by 11.

6. Find the remainder.

7. Subtract the remainder from 11.

8. This gives the final digit.

9. If the remainder is 10 then an X is used and if there is no remainder a 0 is used.

10. Place this digit at the end of the code as the check digit.

**Worked example**

Find the modulus check digit required for the code 3206736 and write the complete 8-digit code. **(4 marks)**

| Digit | 3 | 2 | 0 | 6 | 7 | 3 | 6 |
|---|---|---|---|---|---|---|---|
| Weighting | 8 | 7 | 6 | 5 | 4 | 3 | 2 |
| Digit × weighting | 24 | 14 | 0 | 30 | 28 | 9 | 12 |

Total = 24 + 14 + 30 + 28 + 9 + 12

     = 117

117 ÷ 11 = 10 with a remainder of **7**

    11 − 7 = **4**

The check digit is 4, so the 8-digit code is 32067364

## Using check digits to check the code

If a modulus 11 check digit is used, the code will be divisible by 11 with no remainder.
To check a code:

1. Give each digit a weighting, starting with 1, from right to left.

2. Multiply each digit by its weighting.

3. Find the total.

4. Divide the total by 11.

5. If there is no remainder, it is a valid code.

This is a **validation check** and shows if the number entered is a **valid** code. It does not show that it is the **correct** code for the item in question.

**Worked example**

A bank account number has a modulus 11 check digit. The account number 21336237 is entered. Is this a valid number? **(4 marks)**

| Digit | 2 | 1 | 3 | 3 | 6 | 2 | 3 | 7 |
|---|---|---|---|---|---|---|---|---|
| Weighting | 8 | 7 | 6 | 5 | 4 | 3 | 2 | 1 |
| Digit × weighting | 16 | 7 | 18 | 15 | 24 | 6 | 6 | 7 |

Total = 16 + 7 + 18 + 15 + 24 + 6 + 6 + 7 = 99

99 ÷ 11 = 9 with no remainder.

Therefore it is a valid code.

**Now try this**

A bank account number is given the following 7-digit number: 3567936.

Calculate the modulus 11 check digit and write the complete 8-digit account number. **(4 marks)**

# Characters

Computers represent text characters, numbers and symbols in binary as strings of 1s and 0s.

## ASCII code

- Text and characters are represented by the **ASCII** code (American Standard Code for Information Interchange).

- ASCII is a **7-bit code**. There are **128** ($2^7$) code sequences representing English characters and control actions such as SPACE and SHIFT.

> The ASCII code for the letter C is 1000011 (67 in denary). The ASCII code for the control action SPACE is 0100000 (32 in denary).

- The **character set** is the list of binary codes that can be recognised by the computer hardware and software.

## ASCII code groups

ASCII codes are grouped according to function.

| 0–32 | Control codes, e.g. SHIFT, SPACE |
|---|---|
| 33–47 | Symbols, e.g. (, !, * |
| 48–57 | Digits 0 to 9 |
| 58–64 | Symbols, e.g. @ < > |
| 65–90 | Upper case characters, e.g. A, Z |
| 91–96 | Symbols, e.g. [ , \, ] |
| 97–122 | Lower case characters, e.g. a, z |
| 123–127 | Symbols, e.g. {, DEL, } |

## Extended ASCII code

- The extended ASCII uses **8 bits**, so there are **256** ($2^8$) code sequences.

- It includes mathematical characters such as $\pi$ and symbols for graphics.

- It has not been standardised in the same way as the 7-bit code has and different manufacturers use different codes for different characters. Data cannot be transferred across platforms accurately.

- There are not enough codes to represent different languages.

## Unicode

Unicode has become the universal standard recognised and used by the major hardware and software manufacturers. It can represent text in all known human languages. Unicode can use up to 32 bits to represent over 1 million characters. The first 128 characters of Unicode correspond to 7-bit ASCII.

## ASCII codes in pseudocode

Programming languages have functions to return the ASCII code (in denary) for characters and also to return the character from the denary code.

In the OCR pseudocode, these functions are ASC() and CHR(), e.g.

- ASC(C) would return the number '67'
- CHR(68) would return the character 'D'.

### Worked example

The following string was assigned to the variable named myString:

```
myString = "Once upon a time."
```

(a) Using pseudocode, write a program that will print the ASCII codes for each of the characters in the string. **(2 marks)**

```
for index = 0  to myString.length - 1
  print(ASC(myString(index))
next index
```

> Remember that the indexing of strings starts at 0 and not 1.

(b) The character at index(2) returns the number 99 and index(3) returns 101. State the number that will be returned at index (8). **(1 mark)**

110

> Lower case characters are in the range 97–122. The letter 'c', at index (2) is 99 and 'e' is 101. Therefore the letter 'n' will be 110 as 'n' is nine places further along in the alphabet than 'e'. Don't forget to count the spaces!

### Now try this

Using pseudocode, write a program that will return the 7-bit ASCII character for a denary number entered by a user. Remember to use validation to prevent a user from entering an invalid number. **(4 marks)**

# Images

In a computer all images are represented as strings of 1s and 0s.

## Pixels

A digital image is composed of many small points of colour. Each one is called a **pixel** (short for **pic**ture **el**ement). Each pixel has its own individual colour. The greater the number of pixels, the greater the detail in the picture.

## Colour depth

Colour depth is the number of bits used to encode the colour of each pixel.

The more bits used to encode the colour, the greater the number of actual colours that can be represented in the image so that it is more detailed.

| Number of bits | Number of colours |
|:---:|:---:|
| 1 | 2 ($2^1$) |
| 8 | 256 ($2^8$) |
| 24 | 16 777 216 ($2^{24}$) |

Modern cameras and smartphones produce images with a colour depth of 24 bits.

## Image size

The size of an image is given as the number of pixels in its width (*W*) and height (*H*). When a small image is enlarged to cover a larger area it is less sharp as there are fewer pixels per unit area. It has a lower **resolution**. The resolution describes the number of pixels per unit area.

Look at how sharp the small image is and then how blurred it becomes when enlarged.

## Image file size

- ✓ The size of an image file in bits depends on image size and colour depth.
- ✓ The file size in bits can be calculated using the following formula:

$$\underset{\text{width}}{} W \times H \times D \underset{\text{colour depth}}{}$$

height — on *H*

- ✓ The better the image quality, the larger the file size. Large file sizes can be a problem if they are being transferred electronically or if storage space is limited.

## Metadata

Metadata is extra information about the image stored within the file and can include:

- make and model number of the camera
- dimensions of the image and file size
- speed and aperture settings
- GPS data showing the location where the image was taken.

Take care when uploading images to social networking sites if GPS metadata is included in the file as strangers will be able to see your location.

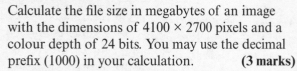

Remember to convert to the units asked for in the question, in this case, megabytes.

## Now try this

Describe the factors that affect the quality of a digital image. **(4 marks)**

# Sound

Sounds can be represented in digital form as streams of 1s and 0s. Sound is caused by vibrations travelling through a medium such as air, water or a metal. Sound recordings convert the changes in air pressure into voltage changes. These are **analogue recordings**.

## Sound sampling

Samples of the sound wave are taken at regular fixed intervals. This is called the **sampling frequency**. A high sampling frequency gives a more accurate reproduction of the analogue waveform.

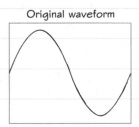
Original waveform

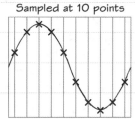
Sampled at 10 points

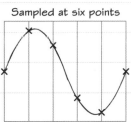
Sampled at six points

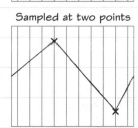
Sampled at two points

The loss in quality is represented here by the shape of the waveform – the diagram with 10 samples is much closer to the original shape than the one with only two samples.

For CDs, a sampling frequency of 44 100 per second (44.1 kHz) is used. A sampling frequency of 96 000 Hz is used for Blu-ray audio.

1 hertz (Hz) = 1 cycle per second,
1 kHz = 1 kilohertz = 1000 Hz.

CDs are recorded in stereo and so have two channels. Therefore the total file size will be doubled.

## Digital sound recording

Transistors are either on or off, and cannot continuously reproduce analogue changes. Instead, digital recordings use snapshots of the sound at regular fixed intervals and then play them back one after the other. These snapshots are called **samples**.

A digital sound recording is like an animated film that consists of many still images with tiny differences between them. When they are played back quickly it creates the illusion of movement.

### Bit depth

 The bit depth (or **sample size**) describes the number of bits used to encode each sample.

 A high bit depth allows more data to be stored and allows the dynamic range of the sound to be more accurately represented.

 Using 8 bits allows 256 gradations of volume. 16 bits allows 65 536 and 24 bits allows for 16.7 million.

### Dynamic range

 The **dynamic range** is the range of volume in the sound.

 The quality of the digital audio depends on the **sample frequency** and the **bit depth**.

 The higher the sample frequency and bit depth, the larger the size of the audio file.

 **Bit rate** is the amount of data processed every second.
bit rate = sample frequency × bit depth
file size (bits) = sample frequency × bit depth × recording length (seconds)
or file size = bit rate × recording length (seconds)

## Worked example

Calculate the file size in megabytes of a digital audio file of 3 minutes duration with a sampling frequency of 44.1 kHz and a bit depth of 16 bits. You may use the decimal prefix (1000) in your calculation. **(2 marks)**

File size (bits) = sample frequency × bit depth × recording length
= 44 100 × 16 × (3 × 60) bits
= 127 008 000 bits = 15 876 000 bytes
= 15 875 kilobytes = 15.87 megabytes

## Now try this

1 When digitising sound, state what is meant by:
(a) sampling frequency
(b) bit rate. **(2 marks)**

2 Calculate the file size in megabytes of a stereo audio file if the duration is 2 minutes 30 seconds and the sampling frequency is 44.1 kHz with a bit depth (sample size) of 16. You may use the decimal prefix (1000) in your calculation.
**(2 marks)**

# Compression

The sizes of large files can be reduced using compression algorithms that repackage the data or remove some of it.

| | Lossless compression | Lossy compression |
|---|---|---|
| What it does | • Reduces file sizes without deleting any data<br>• Nothing is lost | • Reduces file size by deleting some data.<br>• The original can never be reconstituted – it has been irreversibly changed. |
| How it compresses | Looks for redundancy where the same data is stored many times and groups this data into one reference. | • In image files, algorithms analyse the image and find areas where there are only slight differences. These are given the same value and the file can be rewritten using fewer bits.<br>• In digital sound recordings very small variations in frequency, tone and volume are removed to reduce the file size as the human ear cannot detect these small differences. |
| Uses | • Text files<br>• Graphic files with a low colour depth | • Image files<br>• Digital sound recordings |
| Less successful uses | • Audio files<br>• 24-bit colour files | Text files |
| Examples | • Compressed text files<br>• GIF and PNG image files<br>• Free Lossless Audio Codec (FLAC) and Apple Lossless (ALAC) audio files | • MP3 audio files<br>• JPG image files |

These audio formats can reduce the size of an uncompressed file by about 50% and are becoming more popular on downloading websites for people who prioritise sound quality over small file size.

An MP3 file is usually about one tenth of the size of an uncompressed file, so more files can be stored on discs and SD cards.

## The need for compression

Billions of video, audio, multimedia and image files are uploaded and downloaded each day. Smaller file sizes make file transfer more efficient and reduce the requirements for storage space.

The advantages of file compression are:

👍 less internet bandwidth is used when files are downloaded/uploaded

👍 transfer speed is quicker

👍 less storage space is needed

👍 smaller files reduce congestion on the internet

👍 audio and video files can be streamed.

### Worked example

Describe the difference between lossy and lossless compression and give an example where each would be used. **(4 marks)**

In lossy compression, when the compressed data is uncompressed again, it is not exactly the same as the original but the difference is so small that it cannot normally be noticed, e.g. for audio files (MP3) and digital image files (JPG).

In lossless compression, when the compressed data is uncompressed, it is restored completely to the original file, e.g. compressed text files.

Remember to give an example where each would be used.

### Now try this

Explain the importance of compressing files when they are transmitted over the internet. **(2 marks)**

# Question practice: Correct algorithms

Paper 1 may include questions that require you to interpret, correct and complete algorithms. These will test that you are familiar with the three basic programming constructs – sequence, selection and iteration – and can work with algorithms expressed as flow diagrams and in pseudocode.

## Worked example

A student has created an algorithm to calculate the average mark they have achieved in Computer Science.

```
1    total = 0
2    numberEntered = 1
3    anotherEntry = "N"
4    while anotherEntry == "Y"
5      mark = input("Please enter the mark.")
6      total = mark
7      numberEntered = numberEntered - 1
8      anotherEntry = input("Do you want to enter
       another mark (Y or N)?")
9    endwhile
10   average = total / numberEntered
11   print (The average is " + average + " marks.")
```

There are **five** errors in this algorithm. Some are logic errors and some are syntax errors. Identify and correct the errors.          **(5 marks)**

```
2    numberEntered = O
3    anotherEntry = "Y"
6    total = total + mark
7    numberEntered = numberEntered + 1
11   print ("The average is " + average + " marks.")
```

When checking for errors you must read through the algorithm very carefully. Check that:
- variables have been initialised to the correct values
- loops have been set up correctly
- speech marks and opening and closing brackets match.

Pseudocode doesn't normally have numbered lines but, in this case, it makes it easier for candidates to answer the question by simply writing relevant lines of code rather than having to write out the whole algorithm.

## Now try this

The following is an algorithm for a game where a user has to guess a random number.

```
1    randomNumber = random(1, 10)
2    correct = False
3    goes = 0
3    while correct = False
4      guess = input("Please enter a number between 1 and 10.")
5      goes = goes + 1
6      if guess == randomNumber
7        correct = True
8      elseif guess > randomNumber then
9        print("Too low.")
10     elseif guess > randomNumber then
11       print("Too high.")
12     endif
13   end
14   print("You had " + " goes " guesses.")
```

There are **five** errors in this algorithm. Some are logic errors and some are syntax errors. Identify and correct the errors.          **(5 marks)**

# Question practice: Interpret algorithms 1

Paper 1 may include questions that require you to interpret, correct and complete algorithms. These will test that you are familiar with the three basic programming constructs – sequence, selection and iteration – and can work with algorithms expressed as flow diagrams and in pseudocode.

## Worked example

Examine this flow diagram.

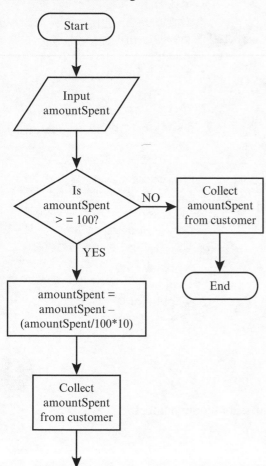

 (a) State the function of this algorithm. **(2 marks)**

The function of the algorithm is to check the amount a customer has spent.

If it is more than or equal to £100, then they are given a discount.

The amount they have to pay minus the discount is calculated.

 (b) (i) State the minimum amount a customer has to spend to receive a discount.
**(1 mark)**

£100

 (ii) State the percentage discount a customer receives if they spend the minimum amount or more. **(1 mark)**

10%

 (c) Calculate how much a customer would have to pay if the amount spent was £150. **(2 marks)**

$$150 - (150/100*10) = 150 - 15$$
$$= £135.00$$

← You will have to follow the algorithm and apply the commands in order to calculate the discount and the final amount to pay.

Practise this skill on the next page.

# Question practice: Interpret algorithms 2

Revise the content on page 84 and then put your skills into practice with this exam-style question.

**Now try this**

Examine the following algorithm. In this algorithm, 'names' is an array.

```
firstName = input("Please enter the first name.")
familyName = input("Please enter the family name")
intYear = input("Please enter last two digits of intake year".)
tutorGroup = input("Please enter tutor group.")
index = 1
unique = false
while unique - false
  loginName = str(intYear) + familyName + firstName(0) + tutorGroup + index
  for check = 0 to names.length - 1
    if names[check] = loginName then
      index = index + 1
    else
      unique = True
    endif
  next check
endwhile
print(loginName)
```

(a) State the function of this algorithm.      **(1 mark)**

(b) State the inputs required by the algorithm.      **(4 marks)**

(c) An array named 'names' is used in the algorithm.
State the role of the variable named 'check'.      **(1 mark)**

(d) State the login name for the following: Rosie Cooper in the intake year of 2001 and in tutor group Red. Assume that her login name is unique.      **(5 marks)**

(e) State **four** facts that you can deduce about the following student: 02GranthamOBlue3.      **(4 marks)**

# Question practice: Complete algorithms 1

Paper 1 may include questions that require you to interpret, correct and complete algorithms. These will test that you are familiar with the three basic programming constructs – sequence, selection and iteration – and can work with algorithms expressed as flow diagrams and in pseudocode.

**Worked example**

A student is monitoring the temperature in a greenhouse three times a day for one week. She has stored the temperatures in a 2-dimensional array named 'temperatures' and is creating an algorithm to find and output the average temperature for each day and output the average for the week.

The following shows part of her algorithm written in pseudocode.

Complete the algorithm by completing or inserting the missing lines of code. **(4 marks)**

```
1   week = 0
2   for day =
3   total = 0
4      for temp = 0 to 2
5         total =

6
7         average = total / 3
8         week =
9         print ("The average for day

10
11   weekAverage = week / 7
12   print
```

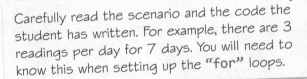

Carefully read the scenario and the code the student has written. For example, there are 3 readings per day for 7 days. You will need to know this when setting up the "for" loops.

Draw a table or matrix to help you visualise how the data is stored.

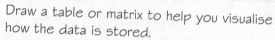

| | 0 | 1 | 2 |
|---|---|---|---|
| 0 | 0, 0 | 0, 1 | 0, 2 |
| 1 | | | |
| 2 | | | |
| 3 | 3, 0 | 3, 1 | 3, 2 |
| 4 | | | |
| 5 | | | |
| 6 | | | 6, 2 |

This will help with the loops that have to be set up.

```
1    week = 0
2    for day = 0 to 6
3       total = 0
4       for temp = 0 to 2
5          total = total + temperatures[day,
             temp]
6       next temp
7       average = total / 3
8       week = week + average
9       print ("The average for day" +
             day + " is " + average + ".")
10      next day
11   weekAverage = week / 7
12   print ("The average for the week is "
          + weekAverage + ".")
```

Practise this skill on the next page.

# Question practice: Complete algorithms 2

Revise the content on page 86, and then put your skills into practice with this exam-style question.

**Now try this**

Complete the following algorithm that is designed to find the largest of three numbers. **(3 marks)**

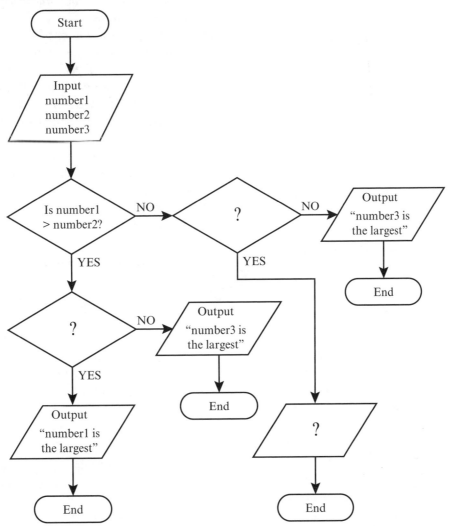

# Question practice: Extended answer question

The exam will include an extended answer question called a 'levels of response' question. This question requires a longer answer in which you have to organise and present facts and evidence.

## Worked example

A small company is bidding for a contract to develop a large system for the NHS. They have never developed such a large and complex system before but have said that they can handle the project.

Discuss their actions from an ethical point of view and suggest why they may have made the claims.

**(8 marks)**

There are several reasons that suggest the company is not acting in an ethical manner.

All computer codes of conduct state that you should never claim to be more able than you are and this is what the business is doing by claiming that they can handle the project without having undertaken one of this complexity before.

Even worse, the business could end up harming people if they do not have the staff to thoroughly test systems whose failure could potentially lead to loss of life.

If the company cannot hire the experienced staff they need, then the project will probably fail. This will lead to a loss of money that could have been spent on patient care.

The company probably made the claims as they are ambitious and want to grow. All businesses must take risks if they are going to grow, and moving into new areas is essential. If they do not take risks then they will never develop and will go out of business.

Although they do not have experience, they feel confident that they can handle this project and so must have analysed what is required and made plans.

If they are awarded the contract, then they could hire more staff who do have expertise in this area and develop the system. They should investigate the availability of staff before they bid for the contract as there may not be any available.

This answer does not include the conclusion that you will be asked to write in the 'Now try this' section below.

## Tackling a 'levels of response' question

This question has no right or wrong answer. You are given a scenario and are being asked to discuss the ethical implications of a company's actions.

For this question you should:

1 Read the question carefully to understand what is being asked. In this case there are two issues to deal with – the ethics of the claim and the reasons for it.
2 Introduce your arguments briefly.
3 Give arguments from both sides. Put yourself in each position and think of the implications for all the different people involved.
4 Give examples to support your arguments.
5 Briefly summarise your points and draw a conclusion.

The student has divided the answer into the two areas of ethics and made suggestions as to why the company might make these claims. They have then discussed the implications of the company's decision to claim to be more experienced than they are.

The student has explained why the company is not being totally ethical by claiming to be more able and experienced than they are. The student has given evidence from codes of conduct such as never claiming to be more able than you are and has explained what could happen if the project fails.

## Now try this

Write a suitable conclusion to the answer, summarising the arguments that the student has made.

# Exam skills: Extended answer question

The exam will include an extended answer 'levels of response' question. This question requires a longer answer in which you have to organise and present facts and evidence.

## Worked example

A school uses a computer system to store all personal and academic details of students and monitor their punctuality, attendance and homework.
Explain how the school should address any legal issues when developing and operating the system. **(8 marks)**

There are many risks associated with keeping confidential data in computer systems, especially the risk that unauthorised people may be able to access it. Keeping data secure is vital. The Data Protection Act stipulates this and other requirements such as making sure that the data is up to date. Here are some of the legal issues and how they should be addressed.

To comply with the Data Protection Act, when developing the system, the school should ensure that only authorised people can access student data. They can do this by creating secure logins and by setting access rights.

The school should ensure that hackers cannot log in by having strong firewalls.

When they are operating the system, the school should ensure that they comply with the Data Protection Act and the Freedom of Information Act.

For the Data Protection Act the school should ensure that all data is held securely and that it is accurate and up to date.

To ensure that it is up to date, the school should send out data-checking sheets to parents and guardians. This will also cover the legal rights of data users to be able to access their data.

The school is not allowed to pass on student data to any third parties.

Under the Freedom of Information Act any person can make a request to a school for access to information that they hold and is not covered by other legislation. Student data is covered by the Data Protection Act and so the school would not allow a third party to see this. The school can show this kind of data only to the individual concerned under the terms of the Data Protection Act.

The school should therefore ensure that all data is kept securely and is only available to authorised personnel and that it is regularly checked to ensure that it is up to date.

## Tackling a 'levels of response' question.

This question has no single right answer. You are given a scenario and are being asked to discuss the legal implications it raises.

For this question you should:

1 Briefly introduce your answer.
2 Discuss the legislation that is **relevant** to the scenario. The Computer Misuse Act or the Copyright, Designs and Patents Act are not relevant to the scenario.
3 Briefly summarise your points and draw a conclusion.

The student shows a thorough knowledge of relevant legislation. Their points are accurate and relevant to the context.
The Act requires the school to keep the data up to date. The suggested solution of sending out data sheets is specific and very relevant to this context of a school's data system.

The student has addressed how the system should be developed and the safeguards that are needed and has then explained what the school should do to comply with the relevant legislation that they have named.

## Now try this

There has been a large increase in the use of surveillance cameras in our towns and cities. Many people oppose their use but others claim they are of benefit to society. Discuss the benefits and drawbacks of CCTV cameras. **(8 marks)**

# Glossary

**Abstraction**

The process of removing unnecessary details so that only the main, important points remain.

**Acceptable use policy**

Rules to which users agree, to reduce the misuse of computer systems. Often found on social networking/collaborative sites.

**Accumulator**

A register of the CPU in which intermediate arithmetic and logic results are stored.

**Algorithm**

A step-by-step procedure for solving problems that can be followed by humans and computers.

**Alpha testing**

Initial testing done by the programmer.

**ALU**

A digital circuit in the CPU used to perform arithmetic and logic operations.

**Antivirus software**

Software designed to prevent, detect and remove malware.

**Application (Application software)**

Software that helps users perform particular tasks.

**Argument**

Data passed to a sub-program (subroutine) by the main program.

**Array**

A data structure that contains many items of data of the same type. The data is indexed so that a particular item of data can be easily found.

**Assembler**

A program that translates assembly language into machine code.

**Assigning**

Giving a value to a variable.

**Authentication**

Confirmation that a user's password has been entered correctly.

**Backup**

A copy of data that is made in case the original data is lost or damaged. The backup can be used to restore the original data.

**Bandwidth**

The amount of data that can fit through an internet connection. Bandwidth is measured in bits per second (bps). This indicates the number of bits of information that can fit down the line in one second. Kbps means thousands of bits per second; Mbps means millions of bits per second.

**Base 10**

Each place value is ten times bigger than the place to its right.

**Base 2**

Each place value is two times bigger than the place to its right.

**Beta testing**

Second stage of testing done by a selected group of users to give feedback about how well a program works.

**Binary digits (bit)**

Either 1 or 0. Computers can only communicate in 0s and 1s; series of 0s and 1s represent the codes for various instructions and data.

**Bit rate**

The number of bits that are conveyed or processed per unit of time.

**Blu-ray**

An optical disc that enables the recording, rewriting and playback of high-definition video and the storing of large amounts of data. It has more than five times the storage capacity of traditional DVDs and can hold up to 25 GB on a single-layer disc and 50 GB on a dual-layer disc.

**Boolean**

A data type, having two values usually denoted as true and false.

**Boundary test**

Test in which the highest or lowest acceptable values are entered; these help to check any logical errors that may have been introduced using the <= and >= operators.

**Broadband**

A high-speed connection to the internet.

**Brute force attack**

A trial and error method used by application programs to decode encrypted data such as passwords.

**Bubble sort**

A simple sorting algorithm that repeatedly steps through the list to be sorted, compares each pair of adjacent items and swaps them if they are in the wrong order.

**Bus**

Electrical connectors carrying data from one component to another or a number of tracks on a printed circuit board (PCB) fulfilling the same function.

**Byte**

Group of eight bits.

**Cache**

A high-speed storage mechanism for frequently-used data. It can be part of memory or located on a storage device.

**Call**

Sub-programs are called by the main program.

**Casting**

Converting one data type to another.

**Central processing unit**

Component of a computer that controls other devices, executes instructions and processes data.

**Channel**

Smaller sub-ranges into which a frequency range can be divided.

**Character**

A single letter, number or symbol.

**Character set**

List of binary codes that can be recognised by computers as being usable characters.

**Client**

A computer that acts as a desktop for users and which relies on a server for its operations.

**Client–server network**

A computer network in which one central, powerful computer (the server) provides a hub to which many less powerful personal computers or workstations (clients) are connected.

**Clock**

An electronic circuit that regulates the timing and speed of all computer functions. Pulses are sent out to the other components to coordinate their activities and ensure that instructions are carried out and completed.

**Close**

When the computer has finished using a text file, closing it saves it on to the disc for permanent retention.

**Cloud computing**

A system in which computer programs and data are stored remotely on a central server.

**Colour depth**

The number of bits used to encode the colour of each pixel in a bitmap image.

**Comparison operator**

An operator that compares two items of data, e.g. <, >, = (also known as relational operators).

**Compatible**

The ability of a device to communicate and share information with another device.

**Compiler**

A program that converts high-level programming languages into machine code.

**Compound statement**

A statement in which Boolean operators are combined to examine a number of conditions.

**Compression**

Reducing the size of a file so that it takes up less storage space or bandwidth when it is transmitted. (See also lossless compression and lossy compression.)

**Computer Misuse Act**

This law restricts people from accessing or modifying data without permission.

**Concatenation**

The placing together of two separate objects so that they can be treated as one, e.g. two string variables can be joined end-to-end to produce a larger string.

**Constant**

A data value that does not change while a program is running.

**Control signals**

Electrical signals sent to devices to check status and give instructions.

**Control unit**

A component of the CPU that directs its operations.

**Copyright**

Gives the creator of an original work exclusive rights regarding that work for a certain period of time, including its publication, distribution and adaptation.

**Copyright, Designs and Patents Act**

This law protects people's original work from being used without their permission.

**Data**

Symbols, characters, images and numbers are all types of data. When data is processed and acquires meaning it becomes information. Computers process data to produce information.

## Data Protection Act

This law regulates how personal information is used and protects against misuse of personal details.

## Decimal/denary

A base-2 number system using two digits, 1 and 0.

## Decision

When a question is asked (as in selection) the answer will lead to one or more different alternative actions.

## Decomposition

The breaking down of a large problem into smaller sub-problems that are easier to solve. An example of divide and conquer.

## Defragmentation

Rearranging the separate (non-contiguous) parts of a file on a storage device so that they are stored together (contiguous) for faster access.

## Denial of service attack

An attack on a network or website designed to make the website grind to a halt by flooding it with useless network communications such as repeated login requests.

## Digital

Representing data in a discrete numerical form.

## Digital divide

Unequal access to computer science technologies for individuals or groups, usually due to financial, geographic, health or cultural reasons.

## DNS

Domain Name Service – resolves domain names into their IP addresses.

## Download

Transfer of a file, e.g. a video, from a central computer to your computer.

## Driver

A program called by a peripheral manager to operate devices (such as a printer or mouse) when the devices are needed.

## Dry run

A program is run on paper and each stage is carefully analysed to see what values the various variables, inputs and outputs have. At this stage, a computer is not being used.

## Dynamic array

An array that has not had its size predefined and can change as data is appended.

## Efficiency

A measure of how successfully and quickly an action is carried out. For a computer program it can be assessed by:
- how long it takes a program to generate a result
- how much code has been written to generate the result
- how much processor time and memory it uses.

## Electronic waste (e-waste)

Rubbish comprising of electronic materials, e.g. old computers, printers, etc.

## Embedded system

A computer system built within a larger device to control its functions.

## Encryption

For security, data is translated into a secret code according to a set of rules in a special 'key'. To convert the data back into plain text, the receiver must also have the key.

## Erroneous test

Test that uses deliberately incorrect data to check that validation routines are functioning as expected (sometimes called an out-of-range test).

## Error

A problem in the design of an algorithm that causes it to produce incorrect results.

## Ethernet

A set of technical standards for connecting computers.

## Ethics

A system of moral principles. Ethical behaviour is often shown by doing things that society recognises as being good or by acting in ways that individuals and societies think of as reflecting good values.

## Execute

To run a computer program or process.

## Execution

When a program or part of a program is run by the computer.

## Field

One item of information in a record, e.g. in a record of a car, make, model and maximum speed are all fields.

## Flow diagram/flowchart

A diagram that can be used to represent an algorithm (or any other process) using boxes of various kinds connected by arrows.

## File handle

A label assigned to a resource needed by a program.

## Firewall

A system designed to prevent unauthorised access to your computer when connected to a network such as the internet.

## Flash memory

Memory that can be programmed electrically but then keeps its data when the power is turned off.

## Float

A number with a fractional value; it will have digits on either side of a decimal point. Commonly used to store currency values, e.g. 1.50 for £1.50.

## Freedom of Information Act

An act that creates a right of access to information held by public authorities, which includes central and local government, the health service, schools, colleges and universities, and the police and courts.

## Frequency

The number of waves per second.

## Flash memory

Solid state storage with no moving parts; used for fast and easily transferable information storage in digital devices such as mobile phones, media players and cameras.

## Fraud

Tricking someone for personal gain or to damage them.

## FTP

A standard network protocol used to transfer computer files between a client and server on a computer network.

## Global variable

A variable that is available anywhere in a program including in any subroutines.

## Graphical user interface (GUI)

User interface that relies mainly on windows, icons, menus and pointers.

## Hacker

Someone who gains unauthorised access to a computer or network to obtain data stored on it.

## Hacking

Unauthorised access to a computer system.

## Hardware

The physical components making up a computer system.

## High-level language

Programming languages that are machine independent and resemble human languages.

## HTTP/HTTPS

HTTP (Hypertext Transfer Protocol). A protocol used to request and transmit webpages and webpage components over the internet or other computer network.
HTTPS (HyperText Transfer Protocol over SSL (Secure Socket Layer)). The data transferred is encrypted.

## IDE

An Integrated Development Environment (IDE) is a software application that provides facilities to computer programmers for software development.

## Identifier

A name given to a variable, data structure or sub-program.

## Identity theft

A crime that involves someone pretending to be another person in order to steal money or obtain other benefits.

## IMAP

Internet Message Access Protocol (IMAP) is a standard email protocol that stores email messages on a mail server, but allows the end user to view and manipulate the messages as though they were stored locally.

## Index

A number that identifies each element of an array or string.

## Input sanitisation

Use of suitable programs to remove any inputs from users that could be harmful.

## Insertion sort

A sorting algorithm that inserts each item in the proper place by comparing it with each item in the list until it finds its predecessor or the end of the list.

## Instruction set

A set of instructions for a particular processor that it will understand and be able to process.

## Integer

A whole number without decimals (can be positive or negative).

## Interpreter

A program that will run a high-level program directly, interpreting the instructions and converting them to machine code as the program is executed.

## IP address

Unique software address used to communicate over the internet.

## ISP (Internet service provider)

A company that provides internet access to its customers.

## Iteration

Repetition of a task for a set number of times or until a required outcome is reached

## IP (Internet Protocol) address

The unique address of a computer.

## Latency

The time delay between the moment something is initiated and the moment it becomes detectable.

## Layers

The organisation of software components into functional components, e.g. protocol layers.

## Local area network (LAN)

Network used for data transmission by computing devices with one building or site, such as an office building or a school or university campus.

## Local variable

A variable that is used only within a sub-program. When the sub-program has completed its work, the local variable is discarded.

## Logic circuit

A combination of standard logic gates used to perform complex logic operations, where the outputs of some gates act as the inputs to others.

## Logic diagram

Diagrams used to represent and carry out reasoning.

## Logic gate

An electronic device that produces outputs depending on the inputs and the logic operations it is designed to apply.

## Logical operator

Operators such as AND, OR, NOT, which perform a Boolean operation on inputs.

## Loop

Part of a program where the same activity is specified once and then repeated for a fixed number of times or until a condition is met.

## Lossless compression

A compression technique in which no data is lost. The decompressed file has all information intact

## Lossy compression

A compression technique in which inessential data is lost. The decompressed file does not contain the full amount of information that it started with.

## Low-level language

A programming language with little or no abstraction from a computer's instruction set.

## Machine code

Instructions in a form that the processor can execute: strings of 1s and 0s.

## Magnetic storage

Storage that uses magnetic media such as a hard disc drive or magnetic tape.

## Malware

Software designed to gain unauthorised access to a computer system in order to disrupt its functioning or collect information without the users' knowledge.

## Memory

Any physical device capable of storing information.

## Memory address

A number assigned to a storage location in memory so that it can be accessed (addressed).

## Memory address register (MAR)

A CPU register that either stores the memory address from which data will be fetched to the CPU or the address to which data will be sent and stored.

## Memory data register

A CPU register that contains the data to be stored in RAM or the data after a fetch from RAM.

## Merge sort

A comparison-based sorting algorithm using a divide-and-conquer technique.

## Menu

A set of options to help a user find information or use a program function.

## Mesh topology

A network topology in which all nodes are interconnected and cooperate in the distribution of data in the network.

## Metadata

Data that describes and provides information about other data, e.g. when the data was created.

## Multitasking

Undertaking separate tasks or programs at the same time.

## Network traffic

Overall network usage caused by all of the data being transmitted at a given time.

## Nibble

Half a byte.

## Node

Places on the network where there are items of equipment.

## Open source
Software whose source code is available for modification or enhancement by anyone, e.g. Open Office, Linux, Android.

## Operating system
Software that manages computer hardware and software resources and controls how the users interact with them.

## Optical storage
Storage that uses optical media such as CDs and DVDs.

## Overflow error
Error caused when a calculation produces a result that is greater than a computer can deal with or store.

## Packet switching
When certain areas of the network are too busy to carry the packets, they are automatically switched to emptier circuits.

## Packet
A small block of data transmitted from one computer to another.

## Parallel processing
When the processor cores work on different parts of the same program concurrently.

## Parameter
A variable used in a sub-program to store data passed from the main program as arguments.

## Peer-to-peer network
A network of computer devices in which each acts as both a client and a server.

## Peripherals
External devices connected to a computer, e.g. printer, microphone.

## Permission
A rule set up for a particular file to control who can edit, read or write on the file.

## Phishing
A form of internet fraud that aims to steal valuable information such as credit card details, usernames and passwords.

## Pixel
The smallest unit of a digital image or the smallest possible dot on a computer screen – short for picture element.

## Place value
The value that a digit's position in a number gives it, e.g. (for denary) in the number 356, the digit 5 has a value of 50 whereas in the number 3560, the digit 5 has a value of 500.

## POP
Post Office Protocol – a protocol used to retrieve emails from a host and transfer them to a client.

## Process
An activity that a computer program is performing.

## Program counter
A register in a computer processor that contains the address (location) of the next instruction to be executed.

## Property
A characteristic or attribute of a data type: for example a property of a string variable is the length or the number of characters it contains.

## Protocol
A set of rules used by computers to communicate with each other across a network.

## Pseudocode
A language that is similar to a real programming language but is easier for humans to understand, although it doesn't actually run on a computer. It can easily be converted to a regular programming language.

## Public domain
Materials that are available for anyone to use for any purpose are in the public domain.

## Query
To search, usually when talking about a database.

## RAM
Random Access Memory that can be used by computer programs to store data and instructions. Data and instructions in RAM are lost when the computer is switched off.

## Read mode
Data mode in which a program can read data in a file but not make changes to the data. Using read mode protects the data file from being accidentally changed.

## Record
A data structure that can contain multiple items of data of different data types.

## Redundancy
The number of items of data in a file that are repeated.

## Register
A storage location in the CPU.

## Resolution
The number of pixels per unit area in an image. The higher the resolution, the better the picture.

## ROM

Read Only Memory – memory that can be read from but not written to.

## Router

A networking device that forwards data packets between computer networks.

## Sampling

Making a physical measurement at set time intervals and converting the measurements to digital values.

## SD and SDHC cards

Secure Digital (SD) cards are flash memory cards that store up to 2 GB of data. Secure Digital High Capacity (SDHC) cards are flash memory cards that can store up to 32 GB of data, so are ideal for video cameras.

## Searching

Looking through a file for a particular piece of data.

## Secondary storage devices

Devices such as magnetic hard drives, solid state drives and USB sticks that store information but which do not lose the data when they are switched off.

## Selection

Process of working out the required course of action according to decision outcomes.

## Sequence

The order in which tasks should be carried out. One of the three basic programming constructs.

## Sequential

Starts at the beginning and moves through a list one by one.

## Server

A computer that provides files and programs on demand to client machines.

## SMTP

Simple Mail Transfer Protocol – a protocol used for sending email over the internet.

## Social engineering

Psychologically tricking people into divulging secret information or doing things that they wouldn't otherwise do.

## Software

Collections of data and instructions to be executed by the CPU.

## Solid-state storage

A type of non-volatile computer storage that stores and retrieves digital information using only electronic circuits and having no moving parts.

## Sorting

Putting items of data into a precise order (alphabetical or numerical).

## Spyware

Software installed on a computer without the knowledge of the user that collects information about logins and passwords and sends details to another computer.

## SQL

Structured Query Language – a language for creating, accessing and manipulating databases.

## SQL injection

A computer attack in which malicious code is embedded in an application and then passed to the database behind the application.

## Star topology

A network topology in which all of the computers are individually connected to a central node.

## Static array

An array of a predetermined size.

## Storage location

A place in memory where a single piece of data can be kept until it is needed.

## String traversal

Moving through a string, one item of data at a time.

## String variable

A variable that holds characters (letters, numbers, spaces and symbols) that are always enclosed in quotation marks. Mathematical operations are not carried out on string variables.

## Sub-program

Self-contained module of code that can be called by the main program when needed. Sometimes known as subroutines.

## Sub-string

A smaller string that is part of another string.

## Sub-tasks

Smaller steps that a larger task might be divided into.

## Swap file

A file kept on the hard drive or other storage device, used to store data and instructions while a program is running but when the RAM is full. Swap files are not as quick as RAM.

## Switch

A networking device that forwards data between computers on a single network. It can direct specific data to each individual node.

## Syntax

Rules of spelling, punctuation and grammar of a language so that the meaning of what is being communicated is clear.

## Syntax error

A grammatical mistake in code, which could be caused by a misspelling, e.g. 'prnit' instead of 'print' or by missing colons, semi-colons or brackets.

## Systems software

Software that operates and controls computer hardware, allows software to run and provides an interface for computer users.

## Table

A collection of rows and columns forming cells used to store data and user information in a structured and organised manner.

## TCP/IP

Transmission Control Protocol/Internet Protocol – a suite of protocols arranged in functional layers used for data transmission across the internet.

## Test data

Carefully planned sample data, used to test programs to check that they give correct outputs.

## Test plan

A plan for the way in which a program is to be tested.

## Topology

The physical structure and layout of a network.

## Trace table

A method of testing that uses a table to show each line of a program and the values of each variable, input and output for each line.

## Traverse

Move through an array or string sequentially one item at a time.

## Trojan

A program that appears legitimate but which performs some harmful activity when it is run. It may be used to locate password information, make the system more vulnerable to future entry, or simply destroy programs or data on the hard disc drive. A Trojan is similar to a virus except that it does not replicate itself. It stays in the computer doing its damage or allowing somebody from a remote site to take control of the computer.

## True or false

Correct or incorrect logical statements, represented as 1s (true statements) and 0s (false statements), respectively.

## Truth table

A table showing inputs and outputs for logic diagrams.

## Upload

Transfer a file from a computer to a central computer.

## User interface

The means by which a user interacts with a computer.

## Utility system software

A suite of programs involved with the maintenance of computer functions, resources, files and security.

## Valid test

A test to ensure that the correct result will be produced with the expected data (sometimes called an in-range test).

## Validation

A process to check that data is sensible and is suitable for use by a program.

## Variable

A data value that can change while a program is running.

## Virtual memory

An application of the operating system that allows a computer to compensate for shortages of physical memory by temporarily transferring pages of data from random access memory (RAM) to disc storage.

## Virtual network

A network that appears to users as a unique network but which is part of another network.

## Virus

A program designed to cause programs on a computer to malfunction or stop working altogether.

## Wide area network (WAN)

A network of networks connecting local area networks over a large geographical area.

## Wi-Fi

A wireless data exchange protocol, similar to Bluetooth, but works over longer distances (short for Wireless Fidelity).

## Wireless access point

A networking device that allows a Wi-Fi compliant device to connect to a wired network.

## Write mode

Data mode in which a program can change data in a file.

# Answers

## 1. The central processing unit

1 Any three from Control Unit, Arithmetic Logic Unit, Cache, Registers, Clock.

2 The clock sends out electrical control signals at regular intervals. The rate of the pulses affects the execution of instructions by the CPU. A CPU with a clock that sends out 2.2 thousand million cycles per second will be able to execute instructions faster than one with only one thousand cycles per second.

## 2. Components of the CPU

The control unit coordinates the actions of the other components of the CPU and the whole computer by sending out control signals.

It also decodes the program instructions and executes them using the other components.

## 3. Fetch–decode–execute cycle 1

During the 'fetch' phase of the fetch–decode–execute cycle, the CPU sends a signal to the main computer memory requesting the next instruction to be executed. This instruction is decoded or interpreted by the CU and executed – carried out. If calculations are required, these are carried out by the ALU.

## 4. Fetch–decode–execute cycle 2

- The MDR acts as a temporary store (buffer) for anything that is copied from memory ready for the CPU to use.
- The accumulator stores data as it is being manipulated.

## 5. Performance of the CPU

Not all programs are written to take advantage of parallel processing and some processes may not be able to start until others have finished as they require output from them.

## 6. Embedded systems

(a) An embedded system is a computer system built into another device in order to control it.

(b) The role of embedded systems in real-time applications is to monitor and respond to an external environment by processing input from sensors.

## 7. RAM and ROM

1 RAM.

2 RAM is volatile and ROM is not.
RAM can be written to but ROM cannot.

## 8. Virtual memory

Adding more RAM will increase the number of program instructions and data that can be stored in main memory. This will improve the computer's performance because it won't be held up waiting for instructions and data to be swapped between virtual memory to main memory.

## 9. Secondary storage 1: optical and magnetic devices

Unlike RAM that is volatile, secondary storage doesn't lose its contents when there is no power. This means that it can provide permanent storage for programs and data that would otherwise be lost when the computer is switched off.

## 10. Secondary storage 2: solid-state memory

1 Two from: faster access, quieter, lighter and more portable, solid state (no moving parts) and less easily damaged or less likely to lose data.

2 Solid state storage is currently more expensive than magnetic storage in terms of price per GB but the price differential is shrinking.

Other answers could have included: maximum storage capacity available is lower than that provided by modern magnetic disc drives or has a shorter life span than a hard disc drive.

## 11. Storage 3: capacity, speed and cost

Any three from:

SSDs have faster data access speeds than hard disc drives.

SSDs have no moving parts and are not damaged if the computer is moved or dropped.

The storage capacity of SSDs is rapidly increasing and the cost is falling.

SSDs have lower power consumption and make the computer more energy efficient.

SSDs are quieter as there are no rotating metal platters.

## 12. Storage 4: portability, durability and reliability

Any four from the following options.

- Speed.
- Portability.
- Durability.
- Reliability.

## 13. Networks 1: LANs and WANs

Each shop would have its own local area network and these would be connected to form a WAN as they are spread over a large geographical area.

## 14. Networks 2: client–server and peer-to-peer

There should be at least three points for each network. Benefits include:

- There is no need for an expensive server, which is required for a client–server network.
- There is no need for an expensive operating system, which is required for a client–server network.
- There is no need for trained staff, who are required for a client–server network.
- A peer-to-peer network is much easier to set up and requires less specialist knowledge.

Drawbacks include:

- A peer-to-peer network is less secure as login names and passwords are not centrally managed on the server as they are in a client–server network.
- Files are not centrally stored but are distributed throughout the network.
- Files cannot be centrally backed up but, on a peer-to-peer network, each client has to be backed up separately.
- Client machines may start to run slowly if other users are accessing files or software on them or using peripherals attached to them.

## 15. Transmission media

There should be at least three points for each transmission medium.

Wired network:

- Has a higher bandwidth and more suitable for multimedia used in schools.
- Delays in lessons would be unacceptable and the higher bandwidth will prevent this.
- Better security and easier for the school to monitor how students are using the network.
- No interference caused by walls and other electronic devices.

Wireless networks:

- Students can use their own portable devices.
- It allows devices to be used in outside lessons, e.g. in PE.
- It is easier and cheaper to network new areas.
- Less disruption during installation as no drilling is required for installation of cables.
- Devices that do not have network ports, e.g. mobile phones and tablets can connect to the network.
- Students and teachers can remain connected as they move from room to room.

## 16. Connecting computers to a LAN

Each device on a network has a unique MAC address. A switch reads the address information in the message and relays the message only to the computer with that address.

## 17. The internet

1 Domain names are easier for humans to remember and use than IP addresses, which are either 32 or 128 bit numbers.

2 When a browser requests access to a host using its domain name, the client computer sends a request to a server of the domain name service (DNS) to resolve it into the numerical IP address. The DNS servers store databases of these domain names. If the one contacted cannot resolve the domain name, it sends a request to another. The IP address is returned to the host computer that can then contact the host.

## 18. Network topologies

1 A network topology describes how the devices are arranged on a network and connected together.

2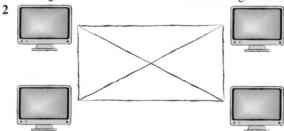

Each of the computers is connected to all of the others. Every computer sends its own signals but also relays data from the others.

3 Adding more devices will not slow the data transmission as all nodes help to transmit the data.

## 19. Protocols 1: browsers and email clients

Both POP and IMAP are protocols for receiving emails. Using the POP protocol, the emails are downloaded onto the client computer. A benefit of this is that the emails can be read offline and when there is no connection to the host.

Using the IMAP protocol, the messages are read on the server and are not downloaded to a client machine. A benefit of this is that the emails can be read from different devices.

## 20. Protocols 2: network layers

A network protocol is a set of rules governing communication on a network. A protocol stack is a hierarchical set of network protocol layers that work together, with each layer supporting the one above it and using the one below it.

## 21. Protocols 3: benefits to specific layers

- Allocating specific tasks to specific layers makes it easier to identify and correct networking errors and problems.
- The overall model is simplified and is easier to understand by dividing it into functional parts.
- Each layer is self-contained, so that a layer can be taken out and edited without affecting other layers in the stack
- It promotes interoperability by providing a universal standard for hardware and software manufacturers to follow.

## 22. Packets and packet switching

Advantages:
- If the backup is stored at the site of the original data then both would be destroyed if there was a fire or other problem at the site. It is therefore more secure if cloud storage is used.
- The data can be accessed from anywhere in the world with an internet connection.
- No need to buy an expensive storage device.
- Many users can access the data and collaborate with each other from anywhere in the world.
- There's no need for an organisation to employ technicians to manage local storage equipment.

Disadvantages:
- Needs an internet connection.
- Download and upload speeds can be affected by the internet connection.
- The hosting company could be targeted by online hackers.
- You have less control if the data is held by another company.
- Storing some data online may breach the Data Protection Act as it should be kept secure and confidential.

## 23. Threats to networks 1: people as the weak point

1 Social engineering is the act of finding out a person's sensitive information such as login names, passwords and credit card numbers by tricking them into divulging it or by observing them.
2 Two social engineering techniques are:
Blagging – these are confidence tricks. The blagger invents a scenario and contacts the victim in person, by email or telephone. They invent a scenario and persuade the victim to divulge the information they want.
Phishing – criminals send emails claiming to be from a bank or building society e-commerce site. They ask the recipient to respond giving details of their passwords and credit cards.
OR
Shouldering – this involves watching a user to find out their passwords or PINs (personal identification numbers). It can be done from a distance using binoculars or by using concealed cameras.

## 24. Threats to networks 2: malware

Any five from the following options.
- Install antivirus software and ensure that it is constantly updated.
- Ensure that the antivirus software can scan emails.
- Use adware removal software.
- Install anti-spyware protection software that removes or blocks spyware.
- Avoid opening emails and attachments from unknown sources.
- Install a firewall to ensure that software is not downloaded without your knowledge.
- Ensure that the operating system is up to date.
- Install the latest security updates.

## 25. Threats to networks 3: network security

This type of attack is designed to make a network or website grind to a halt by flooding it with useless network communications, such as repeated login requests.
The criminals use malware to take control of lots of computers ('zombies'), which all send login and information requests at the same time.

## 26. Identifying and preventing vulnerabilities 1

Any three from:
- be at least eight characters long
- contain both numbers and letters
- contain both upper and lower case letters
- contain at least one non-alphanumeric character (!, $, ?, etc).

## 27. Identifying and preventing vulnerabilities 2

- Firewalls prevent unauthorised access, especially from the internet.
- They can be configured to prevent communications from entering the network.
- They can also prevent programs and users from accessing the internet from the network.
- Access to specific programs and/or sites can be blocked.

## 28. Operating systems 1

1 Multitasking occurs when several programs appear to be executing concurrently. In fact, the CPU switches from one program to another so quickly that it gives the appearance of executing all of the programs at the same time.
2 The operating system allocates processor time to the different processes occurring.
The operating system checks that requests for memory space by the different programs are valid and allocates it accordingly.

## 29. Operating systems 2

1 The user interface allows the user to communicate with the computer.
2 A graphical user interface allows a user to use a pointer to select from menus and click on icons within windows. When using a command line interface, a user has to type in commands, e.g. to copy and delete files.

## 30. Utility system software

| A1 | A2 | B1 | B2 | B3 | C1 | C2 | D1 | D2 | D3 |
|----|----|----|----|----|----|----|----|----|----|

## 31. Ethical and legal issues

She could prioritise the requests in the following ways:

Response 3 would be the most ethical as she is considering which would be the most harmful and she is not taking into consideration how much she will be paid.

Response 1 would be ethical in that she is not considering payment but she should also prioritise the seriousness of the problems.

Response 2 would be less ethical as she is considering her payment over the needs of all of her customers.

## 32. Cultural issues 1

Computer science technologies can improve the quality of life in the following ways.

They allow elderly people to:

* communicate with others using email, text messages, video conferencing
* meet new people using social networking sites and forums for their specific interests
* keep abreast of what is happening in the wider world using the internet
* order goods for delivery and services online.

## 33. Cultural issues 2

Internet technologies have had an impact on the ways in which people can access entertainment, especially with the development of broadband.

The computer games industry is expanding rapidly as users can access games online and compete with players from around the world in a real-time environment. Some users earn large amounts of money by creating and developing characters that they then sell to other users.

Internet technologies have allowed upgrades and bug fixes to be rapidly distributed so that users' enjoyment is not spoilt.

Movies and music can be bought online and downloaded from the sites onto a computer or tablet. Users can also stream movies and music for a one-off performance.

Broadband has allowed for the creation of internet radio and television stations where users can listen to and watch streamed content all day.

Internet technologies have changed the ways in which users can access entertainment. They have also allowed entertainment to become more interactive so that users are not just passive watchers but can send feedback and interact.

## 34. Environmental issues

(a) If she just throws it in the bin it could end up in landfill that could result in toxic chemicals leaking into the soil and water supplies.

(b) She could donate it to a charity for reuse.
She should take it to a recycling centre or a certified recycling company.

## 35. Privacy issues

For could include:

* Assist with public safety by preventing antisocial and criminal activity.
* Can be used to help locate missing people.
* If you are in a public place you are already being watched by other people and so why not by people with cameras?
* Recordings of crime can be used as evidence.

Against could include:

* People can wear masks/hoodies to prevent their faces being seen on camera.
* Recorded images are often of too poor quality to be used as evidence.
* People have a right to privacy and to not be filmed and recorded when they go out.
* It is a violation of a person's civil rights.

## 36. Legislation 1

Any three from:

* The customer has a right to know that the data is kept secure.
* It must be used only for the purpose for which it was provided.
* They have the right to look at and check the data held.
* They can demand that incorrect data is amended.
* They can demand that their data is not used for direct marketing.
* They can demand that the data is not used in any way that could cause harm or distress.

## 37. Legislation 2

A Creative Commons licence allows the copyright holders of a work to give users certain permissions. They can be given permission to use the work for non-commercial activities as long as the original author is credited or to adapt the work and allow others to use it in the same way as the original licence.

## 38. Proprietary and open-source software

Professional support will be provided by the manufacturers of the software.

There will be third-party support such as books, magazines and online tutorials.

## 39. Computational thinking

* Decomposition involves breaking a problem down into smaller, more manageable parts, which are then easier to solve.
* Algorithmic thinking is one aspect of computational thinking. It is the ability to formulate a clear set of instructions to solve a problem.

## 40. Algorithms

- Selection in an algorithm is where a decision has to be made and a course of action has to be selected.
- Iteration is where some of the steps have to be repeated until there is a required outcome.

## 41. Algorithms – pseudocode

```
total = 0  //The variable "total" is used
to store the sum of the numbers.
for goes = 1 to 10  //A loop is set up to
run from 1 to 10 as there are 10 numbers.
  number = input("Please enter the
  number.") //The user is asked to enter a
  number.
  total = total + number  //The total is
                          calculated.
next goes    //This closes the "for" loop.
print(total) //The sum of the numbers is
             output.
```

## 42. Algorithms – flow diagrams

Students are expected to use the correct notation for flow diagrams.

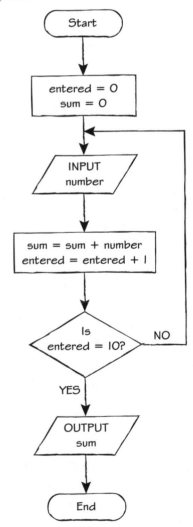

## 43. Standard searching algorithms – linear search

There is no length' method for an array in the OCR pseudocode, so the string equivalent method is used. This will be acceptable in the examination.

```
item = input("Please enter the search item.")
found = false
index = 0
while found = false AND index <= array.
length - 1
    if array[index] == item then
        found = true
        print("Item found.")
    else
        index = index + 1
    endif
endwhile
if found == false then
    print("Item  not found.")
endif
```

## 44. Standard searching algorithms – binary search

The median item is 27 but this is higher than the search item.
The sub-list to the left is used - 3, 5, 9, 14, 17, 21.
The median is 9 but this is lower than the search item.
The sub-list to the right is used - 14, 17 and 21.
The median is 17 which is the search item.

## 45. Comparing linear and binary searches

The median item is 'Mary'.
The sub-list to the left is selected – Alice, Ann, Claire, David.
The median of this list is Ann which is the search item.

## 46. Standard sorting algorithms – bubble sort

The items that have been moved are shown in red.
You will not need to do this in the examination.

| Pass 1 | Pass 2 |
|--------|--------|
| 1 4 2 6 3 5 | 1 2 4 3 5 6 |
| 1 2 4 6 3 5 | 1 2 4 3 5 6 |
| 1 2 4 6 3 5 | 1 2 3 4 5 6 |
| 1 2 4 3 6 5 | |
| 1 2 4 3 5 6 | |

## 47. Standard sorting algorithms – insertion sort

The items that have been moved are shown in red. You will not need to do this in the examination.

Devi Mai Sanjita Alice Maalik Catherine Jane
Devi Mai Sanjita Alice Maalik Catherine Jane
Alice Devi Mai Sanjita Maalik Catherine Jane
Alice Devi Maalik Mai Sanjita Catherine Jane
Alice Catherine Devi Maalik Mai Sanjita Jane
Alice Catherine Devi Jane Maalik Mai Sanjita

## 48. Standard sorting algorithms – merge sort

```
38  27  43  3  9  82  10
38  27  43  3      9  82  10
38  27      43  3      9  82      10
38      27      43      3      9      82      10
27  38      3  43      9  82      10
3  27  38  43      9  10  82
3  9  10  27  38  43  82
```

## 49. Interpreting, correcting and completing algorithms

| number | index | output |
|--------|-------|--------|
| 3      |       |        |
| 4      | 1     | 4      |
| 6      | 2     | 6      |
| 9      | 3     | 9      |

## 50. Using trace tables

| number | index | output |
|--------|-------|--------|
| 3      |       | 3      |
| 9      | 1     | 9      |
| 15     | 2     | 15     |
| 21     | 3     | 21     |

## 51. Variables and constants

Suitable variables could be:
result1, result2, result3, result4, result5, average.

## 52. Arithmetic operators

```
day1 = input("Please enter number sold on
day 1")
day2 = input("Please enter number sold on
day 2")
day3 = input("Please enter number sold on
day 3")
total = day1 + day2 + day3
meanSold = total DIV 3
```

## 53. Comparison operators

```
value1 = input()
value2 = input()
if value1 < value2 then
  temp = value1
  value1 = value2
  value2 = temp
endif
```

## 54. Boolean operators

```
if (cost >= 10 AND cost <= 20) AND (type =
"European" OR type = "Asian") AND distance
<=10
OR
if (cost >= 10 AND cost <= 20) AND (type
= "European" OR type = "Asian") AND NOT
distance >10
```

## 55. Selection

```
charge = input("Please enter the money
spent.")
if charge >= 200 then
  discount = charge/100*10
  if discount > 300 then
    discount = 300
  endif
endif
```

## 56. Iteration

This is one possible answer but there are many other algorithms that could be written. The algorithm uses a random command that returns a random number between the two numbers entered. It is not in the OCR pseudocode but you are allowed to use any commands that could be understood by a competent person.

```
number = random(1, 10)
correct = false
numberOfGuesses = 1
while correct == false AND numberOfGuesses
<= 3
  guess = input("Please enter a number")
  if guess = number then
    correct = true
  endif
  numberOfGuesses = numberOfGuesses + 1
endwhile
if correct = true then
  print("Well done. You guessed
  correctly.")
else
  print("Sorry. The number was " + number)
endif
```

## 57. Data types

- 9
- 999
- 90.0

## 58. String manipulation

ien

## 59. Arrays

```
firstName = input("Please enter the first
name.")
lastName = input("Please enter the surname.")
index = 0
found = false
while found == false AND index <= friends.
length - 1
   if friends[index, 0] == firstName AND
   friends[index, 1] == lastName then
      found == true
   endif
   index = index + 1
endwhile

if found == true then
   print("This friend is already in the
array.")
else
   print("This friend is not in the array.")
endif
```

## 60. File handling operations

```
userName = input("Please enter a username.")
userFile = openRead("users.txt")
used = false
while NOT userFile.endOfFile()
   storedName = userFile.readLine()
   if storedName == userName then
      used = true
   endif
endwhile
userFile.close()
if used == true then
   print("Sorry. This username has already
been used. Please enter a new username.")
endif
```

## 61. Records

(a) A record is a collection of data about a particular object or entity, e.g. a student.

(b) A field is one item of data in a record, e.g. for a record of a student, it could be their first name.

(c) In every record, one of the fields must contain unique information so that the database management system can identify that record. This field is called the key field.

## 62. Structured query language

(a) SELECT FirstName, Surname, Postcode FROM Students;

(b) SELECT * FROM Students
    WHERE TutorGroup = "East" AND SchoolYear = 10;

## 63. Sub-programs 1

```
function analysis(text)
   total = 0
   for index = 0 to text.length - 1
      if text(index) != " " then
         total = total + 1
      endif
   next index
   return total
endfunction
// main program
sentence = input("Please enter the
sentence.")
characters = analysis(sentence)
print(characters)
```

## 64. Sub-programs 2

The algorithm uses a random command that returns a random number between the two numbers entered. It is not in the OCR pseudocode but you are allowed to use any commands that could be understood by a competent person.

```
function dice()
   dice1 = random(1, 6)
   dice2 = random(1, 6)
   total = dice1 + dice2
   return total
endfunction
```

## 65. Defensive design

```
validMonth = False
while validMonth = False
   month = input("Please enter the month of
   your birth as a number.")
   if month < 1 OR month > 12 then
      print("This is not a valid month.")
   else
      validMonth = True
   endif
endwhile
validDay = False
while validDay = False
   day = input("Please enter the day of your
   birth.")
   if month == 2 AND day > 29 then
         print("This is not a valid day.")
```

```
elseif (month == 4 OR month == 6 OR month
== 9 OR month == 11) AND day > 30 then
        print("This is not a valid day.")
elseif day > 31 then
        print("This is not a valid day.")
else
        validDay = True
endif
endwhile
```

## 66. Testing and maintainability

1 Syntax errors are grammatical mistakes in code, which could be caused by a misspelling, e.g. `prnit` instead of `print` or by missing colons, semi-colons or brackets.
Logic errors are fundamental mistakes in the underlying way in which the algorithm is constructed, which often cause unforeseen output, e.g. creating an infinite loop.

2 Computer scientists explain the logic of their code using comments. Programming languages have special symbols, e.g. // that designate that a line of text is a comment and not code to be executed. Indentation is also used to show where statements depend on ones used above, e.g. all the code to be executed by an 'if' statement is indented.

```
If x == 3 AND y == 6 then
    Z = x + y
    print(z)
endif
```

## 67. Computational logic 1

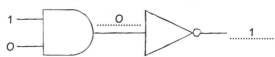

## 68. Computational logic 2

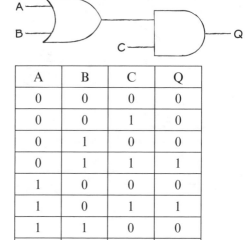

| A | B | C | Q |
|---|---|---|---|
| 0 | 0 | 0 | 0 |
| 0 | 0 | 1 | 0 |
| 0 | 1 | 0 | 0 |
| 0 | 1 | 1 | 1 |
| 1 | 0 | 0 | 0 |
| 1 | 0 | 1 | 1 |
| 1 | 1 | 0 | 0 |
| 1 | 1 | 1 | 1 |

## 69. Programming languages

1 An embedded system is a computer system built within a larger device in order to control it.

2 Using assembly language allows hardware components of the device to be controlled directly. The software will be specific to the particular processor in the embedded system and will not need to be used on other types.

## 70. Translators

A compiler translates the code into executable object code once only as a separate process whereas an interpreter translates every line every time the code is executed. If a compiler encounters an error, it carries on compiling the program and reports any errors at the end whereas an interpreter stops and pinpoints the error.

## 71. Integrated development environment

- Debugger for error diagnostics – this includes use of breakpoints and variable tracing.
- Compiler/interpreter.

## 72. Data representation

1 petabyte = 1000 terabytes
= 1 000 000 gigabytes
= 1 000 000 000 megabytes
= 1 000 000 000 000 kilobytes
= 1 000 000 000 000 000 bytes
= 8 000 000 000 000 000 bits.

## 73. Converting from denary to binary

- 11001011
- 11110001
- 01001111
- 01100100

## 74. Converting from binary to denary and binary addition

$128 + 16 + 4 + 2 + 1 = 151$

## 75. Binary shifts

1 $00010100 \times 2^2 = 01010000$
2 $10001000 \div 2^3 = 00010001$

## 76. Hexadecimal and denary

Each denary number can be converted to hexadecimal.
178 = B2
34 = 22
Therefore the colour would be represented by B22222

## 77. Hexadecimal and binary

        E9
   14        9
  1110      1001
    11101001

## 78. Check digits

| Number | 3 | 5 | 6 | 7 | 9 | 3 | 6 |
|---|---|---|---|---|---|---|---|
| Weighting | 8 | 7 | 6 | 5 | 4 | 3 | 2 |
| Multiplication | 24 | 35 | 36 | 35 | 36 | 9 | 12 |

Total = 24 + 35 + 36 + 35 + 36 + 9 + 12 = 187
187/11 = 17 with no remainder.
Therefore the final account number is 35679360.

## 79. Characters

```
valid = False
while valid = False
    number = input("Please enter a number
    between 0 and 127.")
        if number >= 0 AND number <= 127 then
            valid = True
            print("The character is " +
            CHR(number)
        endif
endwhile
```

## 80. Images

The quality of the image is affected by the number of pixels that make it up.
An image with a pixel width and height of 5000 × 3000 would have a better resolution than one of 640 × 480 pixels.
The number of bits used to encode the colour of each pixel is called the colour depth. If more bits are used, more colours can be displayed.
If more colours are used then very small colour changes can be represented in the image, so increasing the detail.

## 81. Sound

1 (a) The sampling frequency describes the number of sound samples that are taken each second.
  (b) The bit rate is the amount of data processed every second.
2 File size (bits) = sample frequency x bit depth x recording length x number of channels
    = 44 100 × 116 × 150 × 2
    = 211 680 000 bits
    = 26 460 000 bytes
    = 26 460 kilobytes
    = 26.5 megabytes

## 82. Compression

Any two of:
- it reduces the size of the file that needs to be transmitted
- shortens download time
- reduces internet traffic (and hence probability of lost packets)
- allows multimedia files to be streamed.

## 83. Question practice: Correct algorithms

```
3  while correct == False
6      if guess == randomNumber then
8      elseif guess   randomNumber <
           randomNumber then
13 endwhile
14 print("You had " + goes  + " guesses.")
```

## 85. Question practice: Interpret algorithms 2

(a) To create login names for the students of a school.
(b) Their first name, second name, intake year and tutor group.
(c) 'check' is used to count the number of times the loop is executed.
(d) 01CooperRRed1.
(e) Intake year = 2002
Second name = Grantham
First name begins with the letter O.
Tutor group = Blue
There are two other students with a similar login name.

## 87. Question practice: Complete algorithms 2

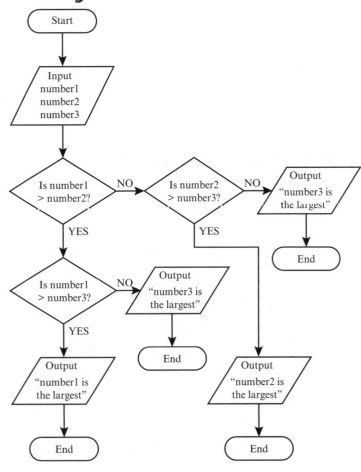

## 88. Question practice: Extended answer question

The company could be said to be acting in an unethical manner by claiming to be more able and experienced than they are and their action could lead to the harming of others.

If they have thoroughly analysed the requirements and made plans for what they will do if they are awarded the contract, then they could be said to be operating ethically as all companies must grow and move into new areas or they will go out of business.

## 89. Exam skills: Extended answer question

There has been a huge increase in the use of surveillance cameras in our towns and cities.

Most people are in favour of their widespread use as they help to ensure public safety.

It can be argued that people will not attack, harm or rob you if they know that their actions are being recorded by cameras and they can be identified from the recordings.

Cameras can prevent damage to property and theft if culprits know that they will be identified by the police and prosecuted.

Cameras can also be used to track criminals who have committed or are committing offences so that they can be arrested at the sites of their crimes.

The cameras therefore prevent crime and antisocial activity and they make people feel safer.

It can be argued that if you are not doing anything wrong then you have nothing to worry about.

Other people see the widespread use of cameras as a threat to their privacy and give too much power to the authorities who can now track any individual through a city such as London.

People who want to commit crimes can wear masks and disguises and the images produced from the cameras are not always good enough to use in prosecutions.

Others argue that it cannot be right to film innocent people without their permission and keep the images.

People have the right to go about their lawful activities without being spied on.

The authorities could use them to track people who have not committed any crimes but ones who they do not agree with because of their political views or protests that they are engaged with.

Published by Pearson Education Limited, 80 Strand, London, WC2R 0RL.

www.pearsonschoolsandfecolleges.co.uk

Text and original illustrations © Pearson Education Limited 2017
Produced, typeset and illustrated by Tech-Set Ltd, Gateshead
Cover illustration by Miriam Sturdee

The right of David Waller to be identified as author of this work has been asserted by him in accordance with the Copyright, Designs and Patents Act 1988.

First published 2017

20 19 18 17
10 9 8 7 6 5 4 3 2

**British Library Cataloguing in Publication Data**
A catalogue record for this book is available from the British Library

ISBN 9781292133904

Printed in Slovakia by Neografia

**Picture Credits**
The publisher would like to thank the following for their kind permission to reproduce their photographs:

(Key: b-bottom; c-centre; l-left; r-right; t-top)

**123RF.com:** 67; **Alamy Images:** B Christopher 7tr, Editorial Image, LLC 11bl, 12bl, Ian Shaw 35tl; **Fotolia.com:** bandung 10c, BillionPhotos.com 6tr, Oleksandr Delyk 10t, destina 17 (server), Deymos.HR 69tr, Aron Hsiao 9tr, mimadeo 69tl, Primastock 6tl, Rasulov 33tr, Mihai Simonia 35br; **Getty Images:** daz2d 77; **Imagemore Co., Ltd:** 9br, 11cl, 12cl, 35bl; **Shutterstock.com:** Maksym Bondarchuk 6b, Robert Lucian Crusitu 34cl, dencg 17 (laptop), dslaven 10b, Equipoise 8tr, Garsya 8b, Gts 33bl, Iakov Kalinin 80, Vitaly Korovin 9tc, 11tl, 12tl, Kuzma 35tr, Lonely 33br, Mclek 69tc, MJTH 33cl, Mmaxer 8tl, Razmarinka 33cr, Rcosmin 7tl, Huguette Roe 34cr, Sashkin 33tl

All other images © Pearson Education

**Note from the publisher**

Pearson has robust editorial processes, including answer and fact checks, to ensure the accuracy of the content in this publication, and every effort is made to ensure this publication is free of errors. We are, however, only human, and occasionally errors do occur. Pearson is not liable for any misunderstandings that arise as a result of errors in this publication, but it is our priority to ensure that the content is accurate. If you spot an error, please do contact us at resourcescorrections@pearson.com so we can make sure it is corrected.